THE LONDONDERRY
& LOUGH SWILLY
RAILWAY

BY THE SAME AUTHOR

THE LONDONDERRY
& LOUGH SWILLY
RAILWAY

A History of the Narrow-Gauge Railways of
North-West Ireland

by

EDWARD M. PATTERSON, D.Sc., M.R.I.A.

David & Charles

Newton Abbot   London   North Pomfret (Vt)

British Library Cataloguing in Publication Data

Patterson, Edward M. (Edward Mervyn), *1920–*
The Londonderry & Lough Swilly Railway.
1. (County) Donegal. Railway services.
Londonderry & Lough Swilly Railway, ca
1900–1953
I. Title
385′.094169′3

ISBN 0–7153–9167–4

First edition published 1964
New and revised edition published 1988

Printed in Great Britain
by Redwood Burn Ltd Trowbridge Wiltshire
for David & Charles Publishers plc
Brunel House Newton Abbot Devon

Published in the United States of America
by David & Charles Inc
North Pomfret Vermont 05053 USA

Contents

Illustrations

IN TEXT

CHAPTER I

West from Derry

THE SETTING OF THE RAILWAY

Lough Foyle and Lough Swilly form two deep inlets on the northern coastline of Ireland. The former lough is broad, triangular in plan and 20 miles inland it narrows to the River Foyle. In contrast Lough Swilly is comparatively serpentine and sheltered, seldom above three miles in width. Between the two is the peninsula of Inishowen, which ends in Malin Head, the most northerly point of the mainland of Ireland.

The eastern shore of Lough Foyle is in County Londonderry, while County Donegal forms its western shore. Further to the south, the inland county boundary of Donegal margins that of Tyrone.

The city and county town of Londonderry stands three miles upstream from the mouth of the River Foyle. Today it has a population of 54,000. Derry, to give it its original title, grew up at the focus of the land transport routes of the district and at the lowest convenient bridging point of the river.

Derry's hinterland is a fertile lowland which continues westward towards the southern end of Lough Swilly. The northern bounds of this low ground are made by the rugged hills of the Inishowen peninsula, which top 2,000 ft above sea level. To the west of this lowland the market town of Letterkenny is situated in the valley of the River Swilly a short way from the Lough itself.

To the south and west of Letterkenny rise the main mass of the Donegal mountains, where Errigal (2,460 ft) is the highest summit. Fringing the mountains is a delightfully varied coastline, much of it rock-bound with impressive cliffs, but with sheltered tree-clad inlets and long beaches of shell-sand in compensation.

Geologically, the high ground of County Donegal is an extension of the Scottish Highlands and the relief of the two areas has a pronounced north-east to south-west grain. A number of well-marked valleys lie along this direction in Donegal, notably the Gweebarra—

Glen Lough—Owencarrow River trough in the north-west, and the Barnesmore Gap in the south-east near to the Tyrone border.

Although Donegal has no large towns and the nearest urban community, Derry, lies in the next county, it was heavily populated in the early years of the last century. The first official census was taken in 1821 and gave a total of 248,000. Twenty years later the county held 296,000 people. This is equivalent to 160 persons to the square mile, but since about two-thirds of Donegal is mountainous, the inhabited areas must have contained around 500 persons to the square mile. Population increase, common to all Irish counties in 1841, was abruptly halted by the Potato Famine in 1845-7. During three seasons, blight destroyed the staple food of the bulk of the people. Famine and disease followed swiftly and offered a choice of starvation at home, or emigration.

County Donegal was especially hard-hit by the Famine, for the majority of its population subsisted on very small farms. Their standard of living was already appallingly low, and the birth and death rates were high. By the time of the 1851 census, the population was 41,000 less than in 1841, much of that loss having taken place in the space of four years. In the next ten years the total dropped by a further 18,000. From then until the end of the 19th century, the average annual drop was 1,600. With earlier generations settled in North America and elsewhere, the export of able-bodied men and women became traditional. By 1951, Donegal held only 132,000 persons, 44 per cent of its 1841 total.

Today, County Donegal has only five towns with populations greater than 1,000. Buncrana and Letterkenny each have about 3,000 and Ballyshannon is almost as large. Bundoran and Donegal town have 1,700 and 1,100. The rest of the county's folk live in 20 small villages or on the very numerous small farms. There is, of course, no coal and little timber, the only indigenous fuel being peat or turf; fortunately there is plenty of that and the mountain bogs are everywhere marked by the black rectangles of turf cuttings.

A CANAL IS PLANNED

At least since the 17th century the bulk of transport in north Donegal inevitably converged upon the city and port of Derry. Only Letterkenny and the compound town of Strabane—Lifford competed with Derry as trading centres, but neither assumed Derry's overall importance. The low-lying isthmus, six miles across, between Derry city and Lough Swilly was a natural gateway to the west and north and it witnessed much to-and-fro movement along the primitive roads of the mid-18th century.

Attention now began to be paid to the improvement of communication between Foyle and Swilly and in 1763 and 1765 unsuccessful attempts were made to interest the Irish House of Commons in granting £8,000 towards the construction of a canal. In 1807 the Corporation of Londonderry employed an engineer to make a survey, but again no guarantee of financial backing could be obtained, and the idea lapsed for a quarter of a century. Then in 1831 Sir John Rennie prepared three alternative plans for canals and estimated the cost of each to be about £38,000. It would appear that the costs of Rennie's schemes shocked the promoters, and five years of inactivity followed. At least the local enthusiasts had been made aware that any canal would have to be more substantial than a mere five-mile ditch between the city and the Burnfoot mud flats.

By the mid-1830s the canal was thus being considered in connection with proposals to control the strong tides of Lough Swilly by means of embankments and at the same time to reclaim the mud flats or sloblands and so add to the area of fertile land. While embankments and reclamation could proceed independently of canal construction, the canal must inevitably depend upon their existence. First things first; a statutory authority was obtained on 27 July 1838 by 'An Act for draining and embanking certain lands in Lough Foyle and Lough Swilly in the Counties of Donegal and Londonderry'. The seven promoters which the Act named were all Londonderry financiers.

The Act did not provide specifically for a canal; it merely acknowledged that one might be made and in that event 'such Canal, if hereafter made to be continued and pass free of all Charge for the Ground it shall occupy through the said Waste Lands, Mud Banks or Slobs, between the Island of Burt in Lough Swilly and the opposite mainland in the County of Donegal'.

By the 1830s methods of survey and canal construction had reached a high degree of precision, and it had become known that the tidal range in Lough Swilly was twice as great as that in Lough Foyle. Though not insurmountable, the technical difficulties were now apparent. They would have led to considerable expense and the scheme was reluctantly abandoned, which was fortunate for the persons who might have been shareholders. The project might quickly have been outdated by the railway, for by the mid-1830s the Ulster Railway and the Dublin & Kingstown Railway were being actively promoted.

EMBANKMENTS ARE BUILT

The contractor for the embankments and reclamations as defined by the 1838 Act was one William McCormick, a well-known Ulster civil engineer and for some years the Member of Parliament for Derry City. Before many years had passed, financial insolvency had ruined the promoters, and would have crippled McCormick too, had it not been for the intervention of Messrs Wagstaffe & Brassey, a major firm of civil engineers in Britain. As the work slowed, a further Act became necessary to extend the time of construction and was passed on 27 July 1846. By the time the work was finished, ownership of the reclaimed lands had passed to William McCormick, Thomas Brassey and William Wagstaffe.

The reclamation works included the construction of four great embankments, stone-faced and primarily intended to prevent the Swilly tides from sweeping across the slob and low ground. These massive structures exist to this day. The longest of them, named the Trady Embankment, stretched from the shore at Tievebane or Tooban, over Trady Island, to Farland Point, a distance of 3,700 yd. It enclosed an area of 2,000 acres. Inch Island lay half a mile off-shore and two embankments were built to join it to the mainland, one from Quigley's Point and the other from the former Island of Burt, near to Farland Point. These were 600 and 1,000 yd in length. The fourth embankment was some way to the south-west of the others and enclosed 900 acres of slobland at Blanketnook. The long Trady embankment was completed in 1850 and by its position it came to play an important part in later railway planning and construction.

THE RISE OF THE RAILWAYS

While the land reclamation work was progressing, the building of railway lines out of Derry had begun. By 1847 the Londonderry & Enniskillen Railway had opened their line, alongside the River Foyle, as far as Strabane. Six years later, the Londonderry & Coleraine Railway was completed, striking out to the north-east of the city.

In 1845, during the period of the Railway Mania, two railway lines were proposed for Donegal. Neither scheme came to fruition, though they undoubtedly sounded the death-knell of the Foyle—Swilly canal. The *Londonderry Journal* of 23 September 1845 contained a preliminary notice from the promoters of the Great County of Donegal Railway, which was to consist of a line connecting Ballyshannon and Ramelton, *via* Donegal town and Letterkenny, with branches to Lifford and Derry. From the northern terminus at Ramelton it was planned to establish 'shipping places' on Lough Swilly, with steamboat services to Liverpool and to Glasgow. On 5 November 1845 the *Journal* announced that a survey had shown that a capital of £600,000 would be required and the names of the Committee were listed: Lord George Hill and Sir James Stewart, both of Ramelton, Sir Edmund Hayes of Stranorlar, and Alexander R. Stewart, Esq., of Ards House, near Dunfanaghy.

In the same autumn an opposing and even more impressive Donegal railway complex was being planned in England. The *Londonderry Journal* of 29 October 1845 contained the preliminary notice of the Great North Western Junction Railway. This Company's capital assets were to be no less than £1,500,000 and its object was to make a trunk line from the proposed Enniskillen & Sligo Railway, across Donegal to Derry city. The line was to begin three miles from Sligo and to run *via* Bundoran, Ballyshannon, Ballintra and Donegal. It was then to traverse the Barnesmore Gap and descend to the north-east into Ballybofey and Stranorlar. From there it would have run to Letterkenny, Newtoncunningham and Derry. A branch from Letterkenny was to run to Ramelton and Rathmullan. The Company's prospectus mentions the proposed approach of the line to Lough Swilly 'through the populous and fertile district of Burt', while it would 'cross over and finish the embankment at Blanket Nook'. It was planned to establish deep-water quays on the west bank of the River Swilly near the gentleman's residence of Thorn 'thus affording to the town of Letterkenny the great advantage of a Port and Harbour, available for vessels at every state of the tide'. The scheme came to nothing.

CHAPTER II

The Lough Swilly 1852-1880

INCORPORATION

Not long after the eclipse of the schemes of the Great County of Donegal Railway and the Great North Western Junction Railway, the potential benefits of railway transport were again being publicised in Derry and north Donegal. In 1852 the Lough Foyle & Lough Swilly Railway Company was provisionally registered, with plans to make 8¾ miles of railway from Derry city to Farland Point, close to the south-western end of the great Trady Embankment, completed just two years before. During the passage of the bill through Parliament, the Company was renamed, and as the Londonderry & Lough Swilly Railway their Act of Incorporation was received on 26 June 1853. Authority was given to raise share capital of £40,000.

The 'Plans and Sections of the Proposed Lough Foyle and Lough Swilly Railway', deposited in the House of Lords, and signed by James Bayliss, engineer, in 1852, show the line beginning in Derry on the east side of Strand (later Strand Road) about 80 yd from the Second Presbyterian Church. Six and one-third furlongs to the north, the line crossed the road named Strand at Pennyburn and held a west-north-westerly course to the village of Burnfoot. There it turned west and skirted the extensive salt marshes of the Inch Level until it neared the north-eastern end of the Trady Embankment. The embankment, firmly established across the mud and amply wide enough to take a line of railway, provided a ready-made course for it across to Trady Island and beyond towards Farland Point.

Though all appeared set for making the railway, no work was begun, doubtless due to the slowness of gathering capital. An extension of the time allowed for construction became necessary and an additional Act was passed on 1 August 1859. This also defined certain small alterations in the course of the line. At the Derry end it was now 'A Railway commencing at the Intertidal Embankment of the Londonderry Port and Harbour Commissioners on the Western Shore of the River Foyle at a Point One Hundred and forty four Yards to the southward of the Mill belonging to and in the Occupation of Samuel Gilliland'. (The Port and Harbour Commissioners were a statutory body formed in 1855 to develop the city's harbour facilities.) At the Swilly end it was to terminate 'at a proposed Jetty in the Farland Channel at a Point Three Hundred and ninety-six Yards to the North-West of the Farland Point in the Townland of Carrowen. . . '. The line was of course to be built to the Irish standard gauge of 5 ft 3 in., as defined by the 1846 Gauges Act.

Both the 1853 and the 1859 Acts included the usual proviso that, if the Board of Trade subsequently required, the level crossings were to be replaced by bridges. The Pennyburn crossing of Strand, actually lying on the city's access road from the north, was singled out for special mention. At first, a speed restriction of 6 m.p.h. was imposed on trains between the terminus and the crossing. The 1859 Act went further and prohibited the use of steam locomotives over the crossing or 'to propel or draw any Carriage across the said Road by means of a fixed Engine and Ropes, or otherwise by the use of Steam Power, but the Traffic across the said Road and along the Railway from thence to the Londonderry Terminus shall be worked by Horses or other Animals'.

These wearying restrictions could only have been avoided by terminating the line short of Strand Road, for elevation of the road would not have been accepted by Derry folk and carrying the railway over the road would have been far too expensive with the necessary long approach embankments. If the railway was not to suffer physical isolation from the busy quayside, the Pennyburn level crossing had to be tolerated.

PRACTICAL PROGRESS

Early 1860 at last brought progress. On 2 February William McCormick attended a Board meeting and offered to build the line for £24,000. There is no record in the minutes of any other tenders. McCormick's reputation was exceedingly good and his offer was accepted.

On 25 April 1860 Sir John Macneill was appointed engineer, though since he was similarly engaged by many other Irish companies, he would have been retained only in a consultative capacity. By the summer the need for local direction was felt and James Thompson Macky, manager of the Derry branch of the Bank of

Ireland and a prominent local businessman, was elected to the
Board. On 9 October he became chairman; simultaneously the
London Board handed over their responsibilities to a local set of
directors. These were Samuel Gilliland, J. T. McClintock, Bartholo-
mew McCorkell, Joseph Cooke and John Munn, all of Derry,
Jonathan Richardson of Buncrana and Lambeg, County Antrim,

Map of the district around Tooban, showing the courses of the
original L & LSR line to Farland Point, the line to Fahan and
Buncrana, and the later line of the Letterkenny Railway

and James Corscadden of Ballyarnett. After seven unprofitable years
no doubt the Londoners were glad enough to be rid of their responsibilities.

Although neither the 1853 nor the 1859 Acts provided for the
construction of a pier at Farland Point, the termination of the line
there was solely for steamboat connections with the small coastal
towns of Rathmullan, Ramelton, Portsalon and Buncrana. Certainly
neither Farland Point nor its immediate hinterland promised the
railway any appreciable volume of local traffic. There was no village
there and much of the neighbourhood consisted of saline
marshlands lately reclaimed from the Lough. From the outset, the
need for a pier and a steamer service under the railway's control
must have been apparent, but shortage of money forced the directors
to moderate their schemes; on 2 December 1860 it was minuted
that consideration of the erection of a pier at Farland and the
formation of a steamboat company 'be deferred'.

EXTENSION TO BUNCRANA

While their line was being built out to Farland Point, the L & LS
had decided that it would benefit by an extension. Access to Letterkenny
was being handled by a separate concern, the Letterkenny
Railway, and the L & LS were obliged to look elsewhere for traffic.
The east side of Lough Swilly offered a more suitable field for expansion
than the west shore of Lough Foyle, and on 22 July 1861 the
Company obtained another Act, giving them powers to make a
branch to Buncrana from a point on their main line, half a mile
south of the hamlet of Tievebane and a mile west of Burnfoot. This
place was at first styled Burnfoot Junction but the name was later
changed to Tooban, a corrupted version of Tievebane.

The 1861 Act authorised the raising of £20,000 in share capital
and £6,000 in loans and permitted working arrangements with the
Letterkenny[1] and the Finn Valley Railways, neither of which had
by then laid any track.

The Finn Valley were in fact merely engaged in linking Strabane
and Stranorlar, some 16 miles south-west of the Swilly's line, but
prudence had dictated that the Lough Swilly be prepared to meet
their neighbour's possible extensions.

To bring in capital, a Prospectus was issued to the public. Carefully
presented, it went through four drafts before it satisfied the
Board. It contained the results of a census of traffic taken on the

[1] See Chapter III

23 Cockspur St

Feb 17 1862

Dear Sir

I have yours of the 14ᵗʰ with Copy of Proof Prospectus, do you think it will be better to have the Map printed on separate Paper, or Printed on Back of the fly leaf of the Prospectus — I think the latter would be preferable, but it should be done as you think best, please let me know as soon as your Can.

Yours truly

John Macneill

Robert Knox Eq
Chairman Swilly Rw,
Londonderry. —

Letter from Sir John Macneill dated 17 February 1862 to Robert Knox, solicitor of the L & LSR

Buncrana road near Derry between 18 and 24 December 1861:

Passengers on foot	...		5,815
Passengers on carts	...		1,127
Carts laden	...	...	1,402
Horses	...	...	189
Cows	...	...	114
Pigs	...	...	75
Sheep	...	...	75

The statistics were optimistically recalculated to show the possible annual income from this Buncrana traffic:

		£	s	d
5,815 foot passengers, say 3d class at 1/-		£290	15	0
1,127 passengers in cars, say 400 1st class at 2/6 ...		£50	0	0
say 727 2d class at 1/9 ...		£63	12	3
Say ½ ton of goods on each cart, 700 tons at 1/9 ...		£61	5	0
Horses, cows, pigs, sheep carried in the week		£20	0	0
Weekly traffic		£485	12	3
Annual traffic		£25,251	17	0

These gross receipts were equal to £32 per mile per week. The Prospectus went on: 'But assuming it at only one third of this sum, or say £11 per mile per week, the Gross Annual Revenue would be £8,438; and deducting 40% or £3,375 for working expenses, there would be a balance remaining of £5,063 which would pay a dividend of more than 8 per cent on the entire capital'.

Like the line to Farland Point, the building of the Buncrana branch was entrusted to McCormick and by February 1863 was well forward. In the minutes of the 12th of that month approval is recorded of the payment of £75 to Lord Templemore 'for material taken out by Mr. McCormick to ballast'. At the same meeting the resident engineer, Mr Coddington, and a Mr Kelly were asked 'to prepare a plan of a temporary pier at Farland Point, which will form one side of a permanent pier to be erected there'. The minutes continue:

> The contractor is to be instructed to complete the line of railway up to the point at which it joins the pier at Farland .... and to erect stations and cottages at the following places .... that the line may be opened in May, viz.:
> at Harritty's Road—
>   a cottage with wooden shed for shelter for passengers
> at Johnston Road— „   „   „   „
> at Elagh—a cottage
> at Dougherty's Road—a cottage   at Burnfoot—a station house
> the wooden house at Graving Dock to be used as a station at the Derry end of the line for the present.

This entry suggests that some form of pier or jetty by then existed at Farland, though apparently it was insufficient for the railway's purposes. The 'cottage with wooden shed for shelter . . .' which was to have been made at Johnston Road seems likely to have been the original Bridge End station, though this cannot be certain since these colloquial names are not shown on the earliest Ordnance Survey map.

In April 1863 tenders were invited for the provision of a single line of telegraph from the Graving Dock to Farland Point 'same as on the Coleraine Railway, to pass the Government inspection'. The contract was given to the Magnetic Telegraph Co. The directors considered opening at least a part of the line before the telegraph was installed but had it made clear to them by Sir John Macneill on 28 May that the Board of Trade would not countenance such a practice.

By the middle of 1863 the Swilly Board were assuring themselves that their line would be ready soon and on 7 July it was minuted 'that about 15 August be fixed for opening the line to Farland'. Things were in reality far from ready for at the same meeting the secretary was ordered 'to advertise for tenders for erecting a station at Graving Dock' (they must have had second thoughts about using the 'wooden house' that stood there) while 'the erection of auxiliary signals . . . and gates at Pennyburn and locks for gates along the line' were still required. Again, on 15 July the Board met to examine the plan of the new station at Farland, and apparently as a result of what they saw tabled, they ordered Coddington 'to add a story to the station' and to advertise for tenders. No plans of that station are known; it was probably only a wooden shed, and may never indeed have been built. Today there is no trace of its foundations and we know from a minute dated 8 June 1863 that a more or less suitable building was already there, since reference is made to the use as a temporary station house and refreshment room of 'the cottage and offices now occupied by Mr. McCormick'.

On 15 July 1863 John Dawson, the manager, was ordered to meet Letterkenny merchants and to endeavour 'to arrange for the erection of a pier at the Thorn', this be it noted, in spite of the concurrent efforts of the Letterkenny Railway Company to link Letterkenny with the L & LS, their Act for that purpose having received the Royal Assent just two days before.

Not even the two turntables had arrived by the middle of July, and Stewart the secretary wrote to Messrs Lloyd & Foster asking when they would be forwarded 'as they are required to enable the

Directors to open the line'. A month later they had still not arrived and Stewart sent a telegram. From remarks in the minutes, it would appear that McCormick had not even then finished ballasting the permanent way. At the last minute, on 13 August, it was decided to put up a platform at Harrity's Road 'for the purpose of making it a flag station'.

The rest of August went by and then on 14 September 1863 the advisability of the Company learning to walk before trying to run was emphasised by Sir John Macneill. Speaking from his wide professional experience, he sternly advised that 'it would be imprudent to forward Plans and give Notice of opening the line, owing to the unfinished state of some of the Works'. Another fortnight passed, and at last the directors appointed their station staff:

Derry Terminus:

Thomas Porter, audit and check clerk	wages 20s per week
J. McDonald, booking and telegraph clerk	12s
J. Devlin, goods clerk	11s
D. Donally, platform porter and shunter	9s 6d
John Rodgers, goods porter	9s 6d
William Tully, guard	10s
————— watchman	10s

Bridge End Station:

J. R. Cary, stationmaster	wages 12s per week
C. Robinson	9s 6d

Burnfoot Station:

Geo. Thompson, stationmaster	wages 11s per week
Thos. Noble, porter	9s 6d

Farland Station:

J. C. Harrigan, telegraph and booking clerk	wages 12s per week
Robt. Henderson, goods and steamboat attendant	10s
John Edgar, porter and pointsman	10s

It appears from this table of appointments, which is reproduced verbatim from the minutes, that the line was to have four staffed stations. Nothing is mentioned regarding the fate of Harritty's Road, nor whether the halt at Johnston Road had been promoted and renamed Bridge End.

ENGINES AND ROLLING STOCK

Tenders for engines were invited, and on 23 December 1861 Sir John Macneill recommended the acceptance of that from Messrs Fossick & Hackworth of Stockton for two locomotives. These were to be delivered to Liverpool, while the Company made their own shipping arrangements. Perennially short of ready cash, the directors managed to persuade Fossick & Hackworth to accept payment by instalments: a first payment of £1,100 in fully-paid-up shares, £660 cash on delivery and the same amount after three, six and twelve months—a total sum of £4,400.

Shortage of money delayed the ordering of rolling stock. Plans and specifications were before the Board in good time, but on 10 February 1862 their consideration was deferred, and orders were not given for another year. On 16 February 1863, the secretary wrote to Fossick & Hackworth, listing what was wanted. When the quotation came before the Board it was immediately regarded as too high, though by what yardstick was not minuted. Fossick & Hackworth were asked to reduce their quotation by 20 per cent and eventually compromise was reached at a figure 10 per cent under the original offer. Fossick & Hackworth finally quoted in a letter dated 13 March 1863:

> Gentlemen,
> We will supply you with the undermentioned as per your letter of 16th February:
> Two composite carriages of two First Class compartments and a Second at each end .... at £380 each
> Two Third Class carriages with four compartments at £270 each (these all on six wheels).
> One goods break van .... £176 each
> Four covered goods wagons .... £150 each
> Four deep sided goods wagons .... £122 each
> All these to be of the best materials and workmanship and such as we feel will give you satisfaction. Delivery in Liverpool. Payment: twenty per centum in shares fully paid up and the remainder in acceptances of the Company at 3, 6, 9 and 12 months. The last two bearing interest.

The engines arrived in Derry in May 1862 and were probably hired to McCormick to complete the ballasting of the line. Some competent person was needed to be in charge of the engines and on 27 May 1862 the post of driver and fitter was filled by Philip Ellis at a weekly wage of 42s. With a better income than the Company's secretary, who had been appointed two months earlier at £100 a year, Ellis's worth was recognised, but his duties must have been onerous. Philip Ellis grew to be a valued member of the Swilly's staff, his service lasting until his retiral as locomotive superintendent 28 years later.

The gathering together of rolling stock progressed in uneasy stages. Some of the vehicles ordered from Fossick & Hackworth in

March 1863 seem to have arrived in Derry reasonably promptly, for on 1 June the directors ordered the secretary to tell the makers 'to delay sending any more rolling stock at present'. Then on 27 July it was minuted that McCormick had ordered 12 ballast wagons from the Ashbury Railway Carriage & Wagon Co. Payment for these was accepted by the Swilly, and McCormick was asked to pay a hire charge for their use.

Later in 1863, the Swilly and Fossick & Hackworth became involved in the first of several disputes. On 19 November, Stewart was instructed to complain 'that they (the waggons) are not of the descriptions ordered, being totally different and not at all the same as those being furnished to the Dublin & Meath Railway which it was clearly understood they were to be'. After an exchange of letters, Mr Hackworth himself attended a Board meeting, on 30 December 1862. Just what the defects were is unfortunately not told, but for the sake of peace the makers agreed to pay £85 towards the cost of alterations. At the same meeting, the Board arranged to have Hector Connell, a local craftsman, alter the brake van for £2 10s and the low-sided wagons for £2 each. One suspects that Fossick & Hackworth probably knew more about vehicle building than did the Swilly directors and that the complaint was a trivial one, trumped up to try to save money.

INSPECTION AND OPENING

The Board of Trade inspection of the line to Farland took place in October 1863. Their report was not entirely favourable, and over two months passed before opening. On 9 November the secretary minuted 'that as required by the Inspector of the line, an undertaking be given to the Board of Trade that the Company shall within twelve months from the date of opening build bridges at Dougherty's, Bridge End and Skeog Roads, and fang the rails at the joints should the speed exceed 20 miles an hour'. No doubt that undertaking was given in a final drive to start traffic moving: the bridges were never built.

It was on the last day of 1863 that the Swilly at last opened. The previous day had seen the Boardroom session with Hackworth, and one is left to speculate whether, afterwards, he remained in Derry as an interested spectator or returned to Stockton to meditate on how soon his firm would get paid for their engines.

Initially only two trains ran in each direction, leaving Derry at 7.30 a.m. and 4.0 p.m., and arriving back there from Farland at

9.0 a.m. and 9.0 p.m. After the morning train had left Farland for
Derry at 8.20 a.m., the peace of the place remained undisturbed
until 4.35 p.m.

The early timetables contained the encouraging news that 'special
trains would run on certain dates'. On Friday 15 July 1864 there
was a general holiday in Derry, and the Swilly obtained their first
experience of running excursions. A service was provided to Farland
'every other hour' and the steamer *Swilly* plied from the pier to
Rathmullan and gave the voyagers three or four hours ashore.

ON TO BUNCRANA

No engineering difficulties were encountered in building the line
to Buncrana, and McCormick proceeded with the construction on
schedule. Surprisingly, the opening date is uncertain. Some accounts
mention 8 September, but the minutes note that the approval of the
Board of Trade was not obtained until 9 September. The occasion
seems to have gone unrecorded in the local Press, which suggests
that the customary banqueting was omitted. It is doubtful, too,
whether the Board of Trade letter received on 9 September was in
fact an authority to open. More likely, since the line was built on
sand along much of its course, the Inspecting Officer found fault
with the solidity of the permanent way, and while matters were
being put right the opening was delayed.

To work the Buncrana road, two new engines had been ordered.
On 13 September 1864 the *Londonderry Sentinel* recorded:

> The schooner *Isabella* landed a locomotive yesterday which excited
> considerable attention on its transit to the line of the Company, owing
> to its great size and peculiarity of construction. It was made by
> Messrs. Robert Stephenson and Co. of Newcastle-on-Tyne, and weighs,
> we believe, about eighteen tons.

The other machine arrived a few days later, bringing the locomotive stock up to four. But the situation was complicated by a legal
battle, for the Company were in arrears with payments of the
instalments for the original two Fossick & Hackworth engines.

By June 1864 Fossick & Hackworth had placed the matter in the
hands of their solicitors. J. T. Macky wrote plaintively on 30 June
to the builders:

> I need hardly assure you of the desire of myself and the other
> Directors to meet every engagement of the Company. To enable us to
> do this we promoted a Bill in Parliament for powers to issue preference
> stock, and with the proceeds to pay off all our engagements. This Bill

will we expect become law in a few days and I may observe the finishing of our Extension to Buncrana has bared the Company of every shilling they had. This Extension we have every hope will very much aid our undertaking.

In spite of this, on 11 October a writ was served for the recovery of £1,532 6s 5d plus costs. The Sheriff of the City & County of Londonderry forthwith seized the two engines and two of the carriages. The minutes make no mention of the direct effect of the seizure, the timely arrival of the two Stephenson engines preventing the withdrawal of services. The fracas came to an end in April 1865 through the aid of the Public Works Loan Commissioners.

RELEGATION OF THE FARLAND SECTION

Three weeks after the second Stephenson engine had been delivered, the *Derry Journal* mentioned that 50 horses were bringing iron ore from the Castle River, near Buncrana, down to Buncrana railway station for transport to Farland. This appears to indicate that the line to Buncrana was open, at least for mineral traffic, by the end of October 1864.

Of the operating details of the line out to Farland we know little. It is clear from the minutes that the Company found it difficult to integrate rail and steamer services, as the latter were outside their control. The report for the second half of 1864 was gloomy, and a working loss of £190 was reported. It was clear that all was not well with what was now being called 'the Farland branch'. On 17 April 1865 it was resolved to work it by horses, an arrangement proposed by McCormick; but on 25 April the idea was rescinded and steam locomotives again took over. The results for the second half of 1865 were as dismal as before:

> The traffic on the Farland branch in connection with the steamers has not paid working expenses and [the Directors] would recommend that this portion of the line be shut up for the present as they have no doubt that the principal portion of the traffic, both goods and passenger, from Ramelton, Rathmullan and the surrounding district, would find its way to the Buncrana line at Fahan or Buncrana.

Some shareholders advocated leasing the entire system, and an offer was considered from Peter Roe, manager of the comparable Newry, Warrenpoint & Rostrevor Railway, which had been previously leased out. But no agreement was reached. Later in 1865 the train service temporarily ceased between Tooban and Farland, apparently for lack of a regular steamer service. After this interruption, an arrangement was made with one James Corry to provide steamer connections, and trains were resumed. For a time, the future of the branch brightened, and at the half-yearly meeting in February 1866 it was stated that there was actually a profit. It must have been small, for the branch was finally closed in July 1866 and an arrangement made to run steamers from Fahan instead. Corry left the steamboat *Swilly* lying derelict, her boilers unserviceable

At the meeting in August 1866 the Farland branch was stated to be abandoned, though nothing had formally taken the place of the Lough steamer. Some kind of ferry service was being operated from the sand-spit close to Fahan station, and in October mention was made of an arrangement with Mr Batt of Rathmullan House to establish a ferry service across to Rathmullan. It was proposed to run three trains from Derry to Fahan in daylight, 'it being usually considered unsafe to cross sand beaches in the dark'. Nothing concrete seems to have come of the talks, though they dragged on until August 1867. Meanwhile the Fahan beach attracted private boatmen. Though the Company had no control over their activities, they had to tolerate them. The minutes said ominously in April 1867: 'There have been some difficulties of removal of goods to and from boats at Fahan to the station'.

From the minutes we learn of what might have been a resurrection of the Farland branch. On 26 August 1867 there is a note of a proposed agreement with the Letterkenny Steamboat Company. As their part of the bargain, the L & LS were to run a train from Farland with passengers only, drawn by horses and meeting the 8.50 a.m. train from Buncrana at the junction. The passengers from the steamer were to 'be in the train ready to start at 8.15 a.m.'. This suggests that the journey time would have been 50 minutes for the branch. Nothing came of the scheme.

The pier at Farland lay unused and the rails along the great Trady Embankment gathered rust until by early 1868, after nearly two years of abandonment, it was decided that the pier should be taken to pieces and rebuilt at Fahan by the Derry firm of Green & McCool. The Company then had a pier over which, as they assured their shareholders, they would have entire control. They would also be relieved of the expense of working the branch and would avoid a heavy outlay on the permanent way. In the spring of 1869 we find the 'waste ground at Farland' being let for grazing at 30s a year. The rails were left in place for at least 11 years, and it was not until 29 May 1877 that the Board authorised their lifting 'as they may be required for the rest of the line'.

THE PENNYBURN PROBLEM

A week after the opening to Farland, the secretary was formally instructed to tell Dawson, the manager, 'to discontinue the practice of running the engines across the road in future'. No time had been lost by the management in disregarding the statutory requirement, but so that it could be adhered to, McCormick 'agreed to provide horses for the present to perform the haulage between the Engine House and the Graving Dock'. It is doubtful whether horses were used for long. The minutes dated 7 September 1864 ordered Dawson 'to dispense with the use of one horse and one man at Pennyburn', which at least suggests that abandonment of horse working was already receiving attention. Certainly it is difficult to imagine passengers sitting placidly in the carriages while the engine was detached and a horse substituted to tow them down to the Graving Dock station at walking pace or less.

The use of engines soon resulted in tragedy. It was recorded on 28 November 1866 that a payment of £10 in cash was to be made to Alex. McCauley, 'father of the child who lost a leg when run over by an engine at Pennyburn' in the previous month, while a similar sum was to be lodged for the family in a savings bank. Six years later, in November 1871, the directors received a note from Dr Corbett regarding the child Lizzie and stating that her family 'were in a state of great destitution'. The savings bank were asked to pay them 'five shillings per week until the money be exhausted'.

In April 1870 the Board considered a letter from the Board of Trade referring to the crossing of the road at Pennyburn by engines 'for the past three weeks'. The Company replied that engines had been taken over the road for the past seven years 'without complaints from anyone', and that in any case there was no money to build a bridge. Although the Board of Trade reacted to that one by sending Colonel Rich, an Inspecting Officer (who came again in May 1873 to see what had caused a derailment), the practice of running engines over the road went on as before. The Board of Trade raised the matter once more in March 1882, and again the Company parried their thrust and wrote back that they regarded the crossing as 'safe and convenient'. Following this, Colonel Yolland came to report. Once more the Company were referred to the requirements of the 1859 Act, and once again they continued blithely to do just as they had done before. Fifty-five years passed before the transit of engines across the Strand Road at Pennyburn became legal. The

L & LSR Act of 21 November 1918, principally giving the Company powers to build a new station at Pennyburn, also gave statutory powers to run steam-hauled trains into the Graving Dock terminus.

For a period from 1 January 1869, Swilly trains by-passed the Graving Dock station, such as it was, and ran over the lines of the Harbour Commissioners to a terminus at the Middle Quay, a mile to the south of the Graving Dock (see Chapter V).

STAFF

The acquisition of a dependable and properly trained staff was a problem for a remote concern like the Swilly. The duties of employees, once installed, were not onerous but their wages were so low that only local applicants could be attracted. On 21 November 1867, for example, the Board agreed to raise the wages of Catherine Logan, station agent at Inch Road, to 5s per week. Thirteen years later, Mrs White was made the Galliagh Road agent at a weekly wage of 5s. In both these instances the recipients would have been living in a railway house at a nominal rent, but nevertheless their wages compared badly with those of the male staff appointed at the opening of the line.

Drunkenness on duty was a common failing which low wages seem to have done nothing to curb. In April 1869 a complaint was received from a cattle dealer that a guard had abused him and had beaten his animals 'with a heavy club'. Called to account, the guard admitted that he had taken two bottles of porter but claimed that he was not intoxicated and that he had only used 'an old wooden hoop to move the cattle'. He escaped with a caution, but was before the Board again in September the same year for being drunk at Inch Road and delaying the train. This time he was suspended for a week and ordered to give a guarantee under his clergyman's signature to keep off liquor for five years. A year went by before he was again suspended and was called before the directors to explain the loss of a barrel of porter between Derry and Buncrana. He was allowed to resume duty but was fined 13s 10d for the missing porter.

A letter concerning a more exotic disappearance was received in March 1869 from no less a personage than Edward John Cotton, general manager of the Belfast & Northern Counties Railway. Cotton, renowned for his impeccable dress and his grey top hat, was complaining that his basket of champagne had gone missing after it had been placed in charge of Mr McDonald, who had been

the Company's manager since 1867. By the time that the loss of
Mr Cotton's champagne was being investigated McDonald was
being referred to as 'the late manager'.

Shortly afterwards the Board considered the misdeeds of the
Bridge End stationmaster, reprimanded for being drunk and dis-
orderly at Buncrana on 6 July 1871. The Fahan stationmaster, who
was suspended because he 'had on several occasions been incapable
of performing his duty properly', was called before the Board in
1880; his suspension was terminated with the warning recorded in
the minutes that 'he will be dismissed if he transgresses again'.
Fahan was no place for him. The station premises had a bar, fitted
out to offer alcoholic sustenance to those about to face the perils
of the deep, or recovering from the effects of a rough crossing. As
early as April 1870 the Board had primly noted that one day the
Fahan station refreshment room had contained three drunk men.
The stationmaster's vows were inevitably short-lived and he was
dismissed in April 1881.

An earlier Fahan stationmaster had an argument in January 1869
with his opposite number in Derry, F. R. Dawson (who later became
the Company's secretary and manager), concerning the loss of wood
in transit. There was some evidence that the invoice had been tam-
pered with. The stationmaster remained at Fahan until a train ran
into wagons on the main line 'with the signals showing all-clear'.
He was then dismissed, along with one of his porters.

In 1865 Robert Hume was appointed second driver. In November
of the next year the Board 'ordered . . . that the engine driver and
fireman be supplied with two good coats . . . from Mr. McArthur
at 31/6 each'. The coats weathered well, the order not being repeated for three years. On 19 January 1872 Hume asked the directors to reduce his working week, then 60 hours, and to raise his
wages. The wages were brought up to 6s per day, but the Board
considered the hours 'not continuous nor excessive'. In May 1875
Hume resigned, perhaps to better himself with another company.
The Board made no attempt to retain him; in the minutes there is a
terse note saying that 'he put an engine off the road on 29 February'.

The Company's shunting horses were stabled at Pennyburn and a
kindly soul who lived nearby, Mary Scarlett by name, used to busy
herself with preparing food for the animals. She was not a railway
employee, but her work did not pass unnoticed or unrewarded. On
31 July 1879, the Board showed their appreciation by making her a
gratuity of £1.

CHAPTER III

The Letterkenny Railway

THE BEGINNINGS

If the Londonderry & Lough Swilly had been slow off their mark, the Letterkenny were even more so. Their Act of Incorporation, obtained on 3 July 1860, failed to trigger off the usual chain of events and in fact six Acts were necessary before construction was completed. The waiting and the work together occupied 23 years, and the resulting railway had neither the course nor the gauge which had originally been authorised.

The schemes of the Great County of Donegal and the Great North Western Junction Railways were passing into history when on 26 October 1855 a meeting was held in Letterkenny to arouse interest in a company to be known as the Londonderry & Letterkenny Railway. A committee was formed, but nothing happened.

Active interest reawakened in 1858 and the *Londonderry Sentinel* of 4 November contained the following paragraph :

> The public will be gratified to learn that preliminary steps have been taken for an application to Parliament for a Bill authorising the construction of the proposed railway between Derry and Letterkenny. The line at first thought of between Londonderry and St. Johnstown has been abandoned as impracticable and one from Farland Point to Newtowncunningham is likely to be selected in preference. John Frazer Esq., County Engineer, has already surveyed the ground, and his report which is understood to be favourable, will shortly be published.

In the following year the Letterkenny Railway Company were provisionally registered. In spite of the doubts expressed a year before, the course was to be from Letterkenny to Cuttymanhill, near St Johnstown, seven miles out from Derry on the Londonderry & Enniskillen Railway. The bill was submitted in November 1859 and it came before the Select Committee of the House of Lords in the following June. The minutes of evidence contain a brief but intriguing reference to the activities of the L & LS. During cross-examination, Alexander Lindsay of Derry was asked: 'Is it within your knowledge that Mr McCormick and his friends, who really are making the Swilly line, attempted last year to extend it to Newtowncunningham and were prevented by the Enniskillen directors, some of whom are upon that Board?' While a railway line to Letterkenny was needed, it could hardly expect to drive direct to Derry on its own. The high ground between Lough Swilly and the River Foyle formed a barrier to a direct and independent approach to the city. To the north side of the hills the Swilly was *in situ* as far as Farland, while to the south-east the Londonderry & Enniskillen Railway already joined Derry and Strabane. The Letterkenny Railway were bound to have to come to terms with one Company or the other and effect a junction; failing that, one or both of the neighbouring lines would probably try to get powers to extend or branch into Letterkenny.

Map showing the proposed course of the Letterkenny Railway, to a junction with the Londonderry & Enniskillen Railway, as defined by the 1860 Act of Parliament. The Pluck to Cuttymanhill portion, denoted by a broken line, was not built. The solid line marks the course of the line towards the junction with the L & LSR, as defined by the 1863 Act, and completed in 1883

C

The minutes go on to recount that the line was to be single. As regards stations, there was to be 'only one of importance, at Letterkenny', with two small intermediate stations at unspecified places, while 'the arrangements at the Junction will depend on what arrangements can be made with the main-line Company'.

CHANGE OF PLAN

The Letterkenny Railway Act received the Royal Assent on 3 July 1860. It defined the line as commencing 'near the town of Letterkenny at the junction of the public roads leading from Rathmelton and Londonderry'. The bridge over the River Swilly, half a mile from the terminus, was to be lit at night 'for the safe guidance of vessels'. The authorised capital was to be £100,000 plus £33,000 in loans.

Three years went by and no construction was attempted. The projected arrangements with the L & E at Cuttymanhill failed to materialise, perhaps because the main-line Company were making pathetic attempts to run their own concern. The Swilly were already known to be keenly interested in reaching Letterkenny if given the chance, and probably because of this, minds were once more changed regarding the best route into Derry. On 13 July 1863 an amending Act was obtained, giving access to Derry over the L & LS. Only a two-mile stretch of the original route was retained, from Letterkenny to Pluck. From Pluck the line was to run nearly at right angles to the original course, through the villages of Manorcunningham and Newtoncunningham, to join the Swilly's line half a mile from Farland Point. The use, working and management of the Letterkenny Railway was to be allotted to the Lough Swilly Company. Enough capital was obtained to enable the contract to be let to Messrs Greene & King of Dublin.

Of the £100,000 of stock authorised by the 1860 Act, £64,950 was issued. Of this £57,172 was paid up and spent on the undertaking. In addition £23,000 was also spent on the works and secured by bonds guaranteed to the contractors.

At the half-yearly meeting of proprietors on 11 October 1864, John Bower, the Letterkenny Railway engineer, forecast the opening to Newtoncunningham by the end of April 1865:

. . . 'all the land, with a fractional exception, is in the hands of the contractors'.
. . . 'of 860,000 cubic yards of earth work contracted for, 290,000 cubic yards have been shifted from cuttings to embankments'.

... 'of 58,000 lineal yards of fencing in contract, 29,120 yards have been constructed, ready for the wire'.

... 'of 1,629 lineal yards of embankment, 960 yards have been executed'.

... 'of 8 occupation bridges, 2 are in progress'.

... 'of 29 public road, river and stream bridges, 17 are complete, except copings, four are in advanced progress, and 8 have yet to be constructed'.

... '303 tons of rail, 40 tons of fastenings and about 1,000 sleeper blocks for permanent way, have been delivered in the work'.

... 'during the past summer an average of 70 masons and stonecutters, 20 carpenters and smiths, 650 labourers, about 36 overseers, clerks and timekeepers, and about 80 horses have been employed'.

Bower's statistics sketch a picture of considerable effort, and of changes in the landscape along the southern shores of the lough. But shortage of money brought the enthusiasm to a halt.

THE INEFFECTIVE ACTS

So that further capital could be raised another Act was granted in 1866 (a year of national financial crisis) enabling the Company to create additional capital. But the money could not be raised, construction was stopped and the line lay derelict.

Cheque of the Letterkenny Railway Company dated 31 October 1867

A new Act in 1871 recited that the promoters were unable to raise the necessary money for the completion of their railway and provided for the rearrangement of capital. It permitted the Company to borrow on mortgage £100,000 and to create debentures, called 'A' debentures, for £23,000 at 5 per cent, the interest to be a charge after the mortgage. These debentures were to be transferred to the contractors in lieu of the contractor's bonds held by them. The latter debentures do not appear to have been created, and nobody could be got to take up any part of the £100,000 mortgage.

The stalemate continued for five more years before the passing of the Letterkenny Railway Act of 1876. This gave the Company powers to divide the £100,000 mortgage into three parts: a first mortgage of £50,000, to be a first charge, a second mortgage of £35,000, the interest of 5 per cent to be guaranteed by the City of Derry and by certain areas in County Donegal served by the line, whilst it was also proposed to create a third mortgage of £15,000.

FROM STANDARD TO NARROW GAUGE

As soon as the 1876 Act was passed, tenders were advertised to complete the line, which had been lying derelict for ten years. The lowest tender made it clear that the line could not be finished as planned. It seemed that once more the promoters must be frustrated but a solution was offered by the Derry firm of contractors, McCrea & McFarland, who suggested the sub-standard gauge of 3 ft.

Probably McCrea & McFarland's proposal had stemmed from experience in the iron-ore mining going on in County Antrim, 50 miles to the east. A mineral line opened down Glenariff to near Waterfoot in 1875, more or less concurrently a line into Ballymena, and in 1877 another from Ballymena to Larne were all on a gauge of 3 ft. They were not only cheaper to construct, but they could be stocked and powered more economically.

The proposition of McCrea & McFarland immediately appealed to the promoters of the Letterkenny Railway. A bill authorising the change was promoted by McCrea & McFarland in the 1878-9 Session. Opposition was offered by Lord Redesdale on the grounds that the use of a second gauge was unwise, and it was thrown out. It was successfully re-introduced in the next Session and passed on 29 June 1880. The new Act went further, giving authority to the Lough Swilly Company to re-gauge their line, so that the two could be worked as one unit, as originally envisaged.

CHAPTER IV

Regauging

MCCREA AND MCFARLAND

The Act of 1880 included an important provision giving the Londonderry & Lough Swilly the alternative of altering their gauge to suit that of the Letterkenny Railway or of laying a third rail into Derry. Mixed-gauge working would have been expensive and complicated, and quickly it was assumed that the system would become narrow gauge. This idea undoubtedly sprang from the influence and advice of Basil McCrea and John McFarland, already mentioned in connection with the Letterkenny Railway, and the partners in a Derry firm of transport and civil engineers. Their firm had made contact with the Londonderry & Lough Swilly Railway as early as 1877, when they took over the running of the Lough Swilly steamers on the dissolution of the firm of Green & McCool.

Basil McCrea had been born in 1832 in the townland of Errity, between Manorcunningham and Sallybrook, and as a young man had been associated with William McCormick, who built the Lough Swilly Railway to Farland and Buncrana. Sixteen years the junior of McCrea, John McFarland was at first on the clerical staff of the Belfast & Northern Counties Railway at their Waterside station in Derry. At the suggestion of Edward J. Cotton, the then general manager, he set up on his own as a cartage contractor. Later Cotton suggested that he should become the cartage contractor to the B & NC, and to get more capital John McFarland chose Basil McCrea as his partner. Both these men were able, hard-working and hard-headed, and the partnership flourished and expanded.

With their intimate knowledge of railway work, they took an interest in the Lough Swilly Railway, systematically buying up the judgment debts and the shares until they were among the principal shareholders. Although neither of them was yet on the Board they were able considerably and increasingly to influence the directors.[1]

---

[1] McFarland joined the Board in 1884, McCrea in 1897, though he had been 'in attendance' at meetings for many years before then.

Having promoted the bill for the alteration in gauge for the Letter-
kenny line, they obtained the contract for that work and also for
the regauging of the Tooban—Burt section of the Swilly Railway.
Subsequently they built the Stranorlar to Glenties branch of the
Donegal Railway, the Clogher Valley Railway and the Limavady &
Dungiven Railway.

Work on the Letterkenny Railway began during May 1881 and
since the track had lain untended and partly finished for so many
years 'the cutting and embanking which had been done had to be
repaired and completed and most of the bridges and viaducts required renewal before the rails could be laid'.

THE SWILLY BEGINS REGAUGING

The Letterkenny Railway was to join the Lough Swilly on the
abandoned Tooban—Farland section at a point near Farland Point,
at the western end of the Trady Embankment. The place has been
called Burt Junction but it was in fact nothing more than the
boundary between the two townlands of Carrowen to the west and
Inch Level to the east. No train had run to Farland since 1866; the
rails had been lifted since 1877. The Swilly still owned the site,
knowing that it would be needed if and when the Letterkenny
Railway was built. Re-laying between Tooban and Burt was done on
the 3 ft gauge during the first half of 1883, at a cost of around
£2,800 for the two miles.

Meanwhile, work had proceeded on the 3 ft gauge line between
Letterkenny and Burt. At this time George P. Culverwell was both
the resident engineer of McCrea & McFarland and engineer of the
Letterkenny Railway Company. As the Letterkenny's engineer, he
wrote formally on 15 February 1883 to the Swilly saying that he
expected his own line to be ready for the Board of Trade inspection
on 30 April, and asking whether the Swilly section would be ready
to receive traffic on that date.

Early in March 1883 the Lough Swilly directors arranged with
McCrea & McFarland to order narrow-gauge engines. Around £9,000
had been paid for narrow-gauge passenger and goods vehicles, and
there were not enough assets to cover the cost of the motive power.
Always ready to oblige the Swilly, which they practically owned by
then, McCrea & McFarland ordered and paid for the three engines
and then hire-purchased them to the Swilly. Each engine was rented
at £131 5s per month, and they were to become the Swilly's
property when £4,500 plus interest at 5 per cent was fully paid up.

INSPECTION AND OPENING

Culverwell's forecast of readiness on 30 April 1883 was two months out; the official inspection did not take place until the end of June. The *Londonderry Sentinel* gave a good report in their issues dated 28-30 June:

The Inspector . . . was accompanied by Mr. George Culverwell, engineer of the line; Mr. Robert Collins, consulting engineer to the company; Mr. Charles E. Stewart, C.E.; Mr. John McFarland, contractor; and Mr. Philip Ellis, locomotive superintendent of the Lough Swilly Railway. Leaving Derry (*sic*) on Wednesday afternoon on a special train loaded up to twice the ordinary weight for the purpose of testing the iron bridges. . . . The line will be formally opened today, when the Directors, engineers and other gentlemen will make the run from end to end. . . . A number of passenger carriages and goods wagons arrived during the past few days by the Liverpool steamer and were yesterday mounted and sent on the line. The passenger vehicles of all classes are exceedingly neat and well appointed and the third-class carriages are superior in their appointments to those in use on the main line.

. . . Although the permanent way has been completed, and has passed the Government Inspector, there is a good deal of work to be done about the stations. . . . In spite of these drawbacks, the opening was accomplished in a highly successful manner. The first train for the conveyance of the public left Letterkenny at eight in the morning with a goodly number of passengers, and we have reason to believe that there would have been many more had it not been that a feeling of timidity prevented many from running what they thought to be the risk of their first trip. However, about forty passengers arrived safely at the junction in time to catch the morning train from Buncrana and they expressed themselves as being delighted with their first experience of the route.

The *Londonderry Sentinel* contained this advertisement:

LETTERKENNY AND LOUGH SWILLY RAILWAYS.

Opening of the Letterkenny Railway for Passenger Traffic.
On Saturday, 30th June and until further Notice, Trains will run daily as under (Sundays excepted):—

Leave Letterkenny 8.0 a.m.   Arrive Derry 9.50 a.m.
Leave Derry 4.15 p.m.   Arrive Letterkenny 6.05 p.m.

Fares between Londonderry and Letterkenny:—

	Single	Return
First Class..............................	3s. 0d.	4s. 6d.
Second Class.............................	2s. 0d.	3s. 0d.
Third Class..............................	1s. 4d.	2s. 0d.

For further particulars see Time Tables.

Frederick Dawson,
Manager.

Under an agreement, not signed until 16 November 1883, the Lough Swilly undertook to work the line for three years, finding all the rolling stock except the engines at 70 per cent of the traffic receipts for the first year and 65 per cent in the second and subsequent years. Two engines were to be provided in good order. The Swilly was 'to uphold and maintain the railway and works of the Letterkenny Railway', running on each working day of the week not less than three trains carrying goods and passengers each way. The service was to be arranged to be workable by one engine in steam, to be in use not more than 14½ hours daily.

The modest opening service must have been due to the fact that only the *J. T. Macky* engine had arrived. Even at the beginning of December, the Swilly minutes remark that no proper service was even then being run due to the shortage of engine power.

When the Farland branch was abandoned in 1866, the station then called Burnfoot Junction was closed and probably dismantled. It seems strange that in September 1881, the Swilly Board ordered Mr Collins to ascertain where the junction station at Burnfoot should be, and noted that Sir Thomas Brassey would give the land for it free. A contemporary map shows both the original standard-gauge and the later mixed-gauge layout at the station, and proves that the narrow-gauge line from Burt was laid, as one might expect, on the old road-bed of the Farland branch. As before, the two lines diverged at the west end of the island platform.

Burnfoot Junction or Tooban temporarily enjoyed the distinction of being the narrow-gauge terminus, the standard-gauge rails from Derry to Buncrana running along the north side of the platform, while the narrow gauge used the south side. A narrow-gauge engine shed and sidings were made at a cost of £263 during 1884. The *Londonderry Sentinel* reported on 28 March 1885:

> The regauging of this line will commence today at Buncrana. A large staff of men have been engaged by the company, and it is expected that the laying of the narrow-gauge rails between the Letterkenny Junction and Burnfoot will be completed by Tuesday night and the entire line between Derry and Buncrana in about a week. The work will be carried out under the superintendence of Mr Stewart, CE, and Mr Ellis, locomotive superintendent. In consequence of the lifting of the broad-gauge rails, the 4.30 p.m. train from Derry this afternoon will only run to Fahan. There will be no train from Buncrana at 5.40 p.m., but a train will leave Fahan for Derry at 5.50 p.m. We understand that the company had purchased two additional narrow-gauge engines and forty waggons so that there will be as little delay as possible in continuing the traffic when the regauging operations have been completed.

The *Sentinel* takes up the story on Thursday 2 April:

> The regauging of this line is progressing satisfactorily and should the weather continue favourable, there is every reason to hope the entire line between Pennyburn and Buncrana will be completed by Saturday night. The line between the Letterkenny Junction at Burnfoot and Buncrana has already been completed and traffic is now being carried. . . . On Saturday last, the regauging commenced at Buncrana at 2 o'clock p.m. and at 4 o'clock on Monday afternoon the narrow-gauge engine and carriages passed over the line from the Letterkenny Junction to Buncrana, no work having been done on Sunday. We understand that the company are adding to the rolling stock three additional engines and a large number of waggons.

A week after the upheaval was started, the job was completed, about 100 men having been employed. Probably because about half the track was relaid with new steel rails, and the culverts were strengthened, the operation took longer than the comparable work on the Finn Valley Railway nine years later. There, the 13 miles between Strabane and Stranorlar were regauged over a single week-end.

With all their track now a uniform 3 ft, the Swilly's next task was to rid themselves of their 5 ft 3 in. stock. The Derry papers carried this advertisement:

LONDONDERRY AND LOUGH SWILLY RAILWAY.
Sale of Rolling Stock.
In consequence of the Re-Gauging of the line between Derry and Buncrana, all the 5 ft. 3 in. ROLLING STOCK, consisting of Three locomotives, Twelve passenger coaches, Two break-vans and Thirty-three goods waggons, will be sold by PUBLIC AUCTION at PENNY-BURN, LONDONDERRY, on 7th May, 1885, if not previously disposed of by Private Sale. Full particulars in future advertisements.
Frederick Dawson.
Secretary and General Manager.
Shipquay Street Buildings,
28th March, 1885.

The three locomotives to which this refers were two built by Sharp, Stewart and dating from 1878 and 1879, and one of the old Fossick & Hackworth engines. The Fossick failed to find a buyer and is mentioned in the minutes as lying at Pennyburn in 1888. On 8 January of that year, D. Luskey of Glasgow vainly offered £30 for it, and on 2 April an offer of £31 from a James Miller was refused. An unspecified offer is mentioned in the minutes on 17 September from a William McCafferty, and since this is the last time the engine is mentioned, he may have been the eventual purchaser.

CHAPTER V

The Existing System 1885-1900

EXIT THE LETTERKENNY COMPANY

1885 was the first year in which the Londonderry & Lough Swilly had a unified narrow-gauge system, 31 miles long. Although attempts to extend periodically attracted local interest (see next chapter), no further mileage was added until the new century.

The report to the shareholders for the second half of 1885 spoke of 'depression of trade and bad summer weather', but nevertheless stated that new turntables were put in at Tooban and Buncrana, that platforms at Bridge End and Burnfoot were lengthened, and £2,800 was spent on the purchase of six passenger carriages and 16 goods wagons. The mileage worked on the Lough Swilly's own line in July-December was 23,846, and on the Letterkenny Company's line 18,818.

Receipts from the latter were disappointing, the first year's gross earnings having been only £4,000. While this was enough to cover working expenses, it fell considerably short of providing the interest on the first mortgage on the Government loan of £50,000 at five per cent under the terms of the 1876 and 1880 Acts. This unhappy state of affairs continued. Entitled to do so by the Letterkenny Company's failure to repay interest, the Board of Works took over the line in 1887 as mortgagees.

The 'take-over' seems to have begun at the end of July 1887, when the Swilly Company agreed to continue to work the line for the Board of Works for a percentage of the gross receipts, for a term of 30 years. Finally on 17 December 1887 the solicitor to the Board of Works came up from Dublin to the office of the Letterkenny Railway in Derry, and then went on to Letterkenny on the 11.30 a.m. train for the purpose of formally entering into possession of the undertaking. With that accomplished, the existence of the Letterkenny Railway as an active company ceased, little over four years after the line had been opened.

The 30-year agreement between the Board of Works and the

L & LS was based upon the following percentages:

Until gross receipts amount to £6,500 p.a.	67%
From £6,500 to £7,000	66%
£7,000 to £7,500	65%
£7,500 to £8,000	64%
£8,000 to £8,500	63%
£8,500 to £9,000	62%
£9,000 to £9,500	61%
£9,500 to £10,000......................	60%

Any balance from these figures reverted to the Public Works Loan Commissioners.

The agreement would have run from 1887 until 1917, and in fact it did so. But detail is amplified if one may be allowed to anticipate the results of another Act of Parliament, passed in 1896, and giving rise to a lengthy extension beyond Letterkenny to the west coast at Burtonport. Seeing that they would be working the line out to Burtonport if it was completed, the Lough Swilly Company in 1896 made a conditional offer for the outright purchase of the Letterkenny Railway for £40,000. The offer was made on the understanding that a Government-sponsored railway would be made from Letterkenny, but not one from Glenties (then one of the termini of the Donegal Railway, successor to the Finn Valley). The Board of Works might well have been glad to get rid of the Letterkenny line, but they were not prepared to do so on terms dictated by the Swilly businessmen. An offer of £60,000 in 1900 also failed to purchase.[1]

REPAIRS AND RENEWALS

The Letterkenny line was apparently inadequately fenced, and goats tethered to the lineside grass turned their attention to the young thorn hedges. The destruction of these 'thorn quicks' was a matter of some concern in September 1886. The secretary proudly submitted a list of the names of the goats' owners and told the directors that he had fined them 6d each and ordered them to prevent further trespass. Inadequate thorn quicks must have been planted when the line was being made, for an order for 20,000, costing 35s per 1,000, had to be placed with a Stranraer nurseryman in March 1888.

Around this time extensive re-sleepering became necessary and steel rails were bought from time to time to replace the old iron

[1] See page 72, Vice-Regal Commission on Irish Railways &c., 5th and Final Report, vol. VI (1910).

rails. Until 1886 Irish larch sleepers seem to have been in vogue and were costing about 1s 4d each. A change was then made to creosoted Baltic redwood, which must have lasted very much better than local larch and which only cost 2½d to 3½d more in the customary 6 ft x 8 in. x 4 in. size.

LONDONDERRY AND LOUGH SWILLY RAILWAY.

Grand Evening Fete at Gwynn's.
ILLUMINATIONS AND FIREWORKS.

On WEDNESDAY, 8th SEPTEMBER, 1886,

SPECIAL TRAIN

WILL LEAVE DERRY (MIDDLE QUAY) AT 10.10 P.M. FOR

BUNCRANA,
Calling at Intermediate Stations.

FREDERICK DAWSON,
D. Irvine, Printer, Derry.   SECRETARY AND GENERAL MANAGER.

Excursion handbill September 1886

In the spring of 1887, C. E. Stewart, the engineer, had decided that the Buncrana road needed extensive re-sleepering, and he asked the Board for authority to obtain 7,840 sleepers. By this time John McFarland was a member of the Board and although he did not become chairman for another nine years his presence was being felt. He rose to challenge Stewart's request and said that he was determined that no new sleeper should be used unless absolutely necessary. To emphasise his point he walked the line with Stewart on 9 April 1887, from Bridge End to Buncrana, making notes as he went along: only 500 sleepers were issued. The action must have infuriated Stewart (he left the next year), but it illustrated John McFarland's strict attention to detail and to the pursuit of economy, to become a by-word in the running of the Company during his chairmanship.

Indeed the incident of the sleepers was only an echo of an earlier McFarland criticism. On Sunday 28 September 1885 a special train had been run to Letterkenny to take home 26 harvestmen who had arrived off the Glasgow steamer. On its way the train struck and killed a farmer who was chasing an errant calf near McLean's Crossing. On hearing of the matter, John McFarland delivered a sharp reprimand to Dawson, the Company's secretary, for having authorised the running of the special for so few passengers.

Re-sleepering and replacement of the old iron rails went ahead piecemeal on the Buncrana road, with progress dictated by obvious unsafeness. A minor accident due to faulty permanent way occurred near Fahan in September 1888. What exactly happened is not minuted, and it apparently never reached the ears of the Board of Trade in London, but the Swilly directorate appointed a committee of inquiry on 17 September. No notes were taken at their meetings but the outcome was that the permanent way foreman was dismissed, and a foreman inspector of permanent way appointed. On 17 September 1889 another derailment occurred near Fahan. This time an investigation was conducted by the Railway Inspecting Officer of the Board of Trade and his report gives a delightful insight into the happy-go-lucky methods of the Swilly's permanent-way staff. The gang had taken out a length of old rail and were about to replace it with a new one when the 11.10 a.m. Derry—Buncrana train ran into the gap, the engine and the brake-van finishing up, half overturned, against the side of the cutting, with two of the three carriages running on the ballast behind them. None of the gang carried either a timetable or a watch and in a significant footnote to the report, the Inspecting Officer states that he found that the ganger could not read the time when shown a watch. Instead, they timed their work by looking across the water to see whether the Lough Swilly Steamboat Company's vessel had left Rathmullan pier. Unfortunately the boat was late, and the train did not wait for it at Fahan.

In common with other United Kingdom railways, the Swilly was directly affected by the disaster near Armagh on the Great Northern Railway of Ireland on 12 June 1889. That breakaway and subsequent collision signalled the end of time-interval working, and Parliamentary legislation speedily insisted on block working, and on the provision of automatic brakes. Until then, the Swilly trains had only the usual handbrake in the guard's compartment or brake van and the engine brake. The inability to pull up quickly became all too evident on 21 June 1891, when a serious head-on collision occurred between two trains not far from Derry.

The Board studied the relative costs of the vacuum automatic and

Westinghouse air brakes. Although the minutes of 3 February 1892 say that the installation of vacuum brakes was authorised, there seems to have been delay in implementing the decision, and it was not until 2 May that the secretary reported 'that he and Mr Turner had decided upon adopting the vacuum automatic brake, as being the most suitable to the requirements of these days and that orders had been placed with the Vacuum Brake Company for the necessary gear for 6 engines, 18 passenger carriages, 4 brake vans and 4 wagons piped at a cost of £582 10s delivered at the works, Pennyburn'.

STAFF

J. T. Macky, chairman since the formation of the local Board of directors in 1861, died in 1885 and his place was taken by Bartholomew McCorkell.

By this time, a rather remarkable man, James Bond, had been placed in charge of Fahan station. He was more than a stationmaster, for he erected a windmill on an exposed knoll and used it to drive a small electric generating plant. He thereby conferred on Fahan station the distinction of being the first in Ireland to be electrically lit. The ingenious contraption continued in use for two winters, until destroyed by a violent storm.

James Bond again received mention in the minute book in June 1888, after he had written to his directors asking for permission to wear uniform, which was apparently not on general issue. The Board acquiesced, but they were careful to mention to Bond that although the Company would supply him with a cap, he would have to buy the rest himself.

In April 1899 Bond was again discussed by the Board. A letter was read from a Miss Kelly, who had rented part of Fahan station as a refreshment room and bar. She complained that the stationmaster had opened another station refreshment room in opposition. Either the inclinations of passengers were such as to offer inducement to him to own licensed premises, or else Bond was finding time heavy on his hands now that his æolian power station was in ruins. Conscious that Miss Kelly was paying them an annual rent, the Board ordered Bond 'not to open or carry on such business'.

The use and otherwise of horse traction at Pennyburn has been mentioned already. Horses came into the orbit of the Board members three times during 1889. The first occasion was in July, and again concerned Pennyburn where an engine had frightened a horse

Within the image, the following labels appear:

RAILWAYS, 3'0" OR 5'3" GAUGE

STREET TRAMWAY, 4'8½" GAUGE

HARBOUR TRAMWAY, MIXED GAUGE (3'0" AND 5'3")

N

LONDONDERRY & L. SWILLY RLY.

Tooban Junc.

PENNYBURN

Loco. Shed

Level Crossing

Shipyard

GRAVING DOCK STA.

RIVER FOYLE

Tramway Depot

Coleraine

BELFAST & NORTHERN COUNTIES RAILWAY

APPROXIMATE LIMIT OF BUILT-UP AREA

SITE OF MIDDLE QUAY STATION

APPROXIMATE LIMIT OF BUILT-UP AREA

FOYLE ROAD STATION

WATERSIDE STATION

Two level bridge (road/rail)

GREAT NORTHERN RAILWAY

VICTORIA ROAD STATION

Strabane

Strabane

CO. DONEGAL RLYS.

0   ¼   ½   ¾   1 MILE

Diagrammatic plan of Londonderry stations, railways and tramways, around 1900 in the charge of Tom Kelly. Kelly had been injured when trying to restrain the animal and he claimed £10 from the Company. Probably aware of their weak position anent engines on the road, they did not contest Kelly's claim, but managed to satisfy him with the odd sum of £6 1s.

At the same Board meeting, the directors had stationmaster Colquhoun of Bridge End on the carpet, reprimanding him for having sent wagons along the main line by horses. The facts suggest that in the absence of engine power Colquhoun was making admirable use of local resources.

The third horsey incident was formally reported by the secretary in October. A few days before, a train had hit a horse and cart at Horner's Crossing, near Letterkenny. The horse was killed, and a lad Hegarty was injured. Accidents at accommodation crossings, where the responsibility for safe transit rested with the users of the crossing, were of course relatively common.

THE SWILLY V. THE HARBOUR COMMISSIONERS

The earliest terminus of the Swilly in Derry was, as we have seen, beside the Graving Dock about 200 yd south of the Pennyburn level crossing. This station was about one mile from the centre of the city and about 1½ miles from the bridge across the River Foyle. Both the Londonderry & Coleraine Railway—successively the Belfast & Northern Counties, the Midland Railway (Northern Counties Committee) and the LMS (NCC)—and the Londonderry & Enniskillen Railway—later the GNRI—had their termini close to opposite ends of the bridge. Even if the Swilly could have obtained Parliamentary authority to drive their line into the heart of the city, such a scheme would have been impossibly expensive. The only valid alternative route was the recently built quayside, and arrangements were made with the Londonderry Port & Harbour Commissioners, who had been in statutory control of the river frontage since 1855.

From 1 January 1869, Swilly trains by-passed the Graving Dock station, such as it was, and ran over the lines of the Harbour Commissioners to a terminus at the Middle Quay, a mile to the south of the Graving Dock. This was a much more convenient place for passengers to leave and join the train, and the distance to the Foyle Road station of the L & E was reduced by about two-thirds. The new terminus was apparently a large shed near where the Guildhall was built afterwards, though an open platform was used later.[1]

[1] *Journal IRRS*, 3, 212 (1954)

DISSENSION

Friction seems to have begun between the Swilly management and the Harbour Commissioners in 1884, if not earlier. During 1883, the Board took steps to put the old Graving Dock station 'in order' at a cost not above £500, and according to a contemporary newspaper report the new Graving Dock station was opened in December 1883, though apparently only as a goods store.

There is little doubt that the reconstruction of the Graving Dock station was prompted by a foretaste of trouble. The Swilly had paid the Harbour Commissioners £750 a year for the use of their quayside tramway, and rejected a request by the Commissioners for an increase to £860. Matters came to a head at the end of 1884 when the Harbour Commissioners refused passage to the trains by the simple and effective method of lifting some rails at the boundary of their own property. Indignant, the Swilly promptly placed an advertisement in the *Londonderry Sentinel* of 3 January 1885:

> In consequence of the action of the Londonderry Port and Harbour Commissioners in stopping our Traffic at the Graving Dock, we are compelled to deliver and receive all Passengers, Goods and Live Stock Traffic at the Company's OLD STATION near the GRAVING DOCK, on and after this date.
>
> Trains will start from the Graving Dock station as under: 6.30 a.m., 11.10 a.m., 1.10 p.m., 4.30 p.m.

The impasse continued until June 1885, when a new agreement increased the Swilly's annual payment to £800 per year. Two months earlier the Swilly had carried out the regauging, hence when the new agreement came into force, narrow-gauge trains were arriving at the Graving Dock. Since the Harbour Commissioners had already to accept traffic off the Great Northern, it became necessary to mix the gauge of their tramways.

Under the new agreement, the Harbour Commissioners were bound to provide haulage for the Lough Swilly trains. From 1 July 1885 the trains again terminated at the Middle Quay, but were drawn in from the Graving Dock junction by the second of the ex-Lough Swilly, Stephenson-built, standard-gauge engines. This engine, built in 1862 and bought by the Harbour Commissioners in 1883, was in such poor shape by 1887 that it was frequently breaking down. In order to maintain their side of the working agreement, the Commissioners were obliged to hire an engine. They tried without success to get a standard-gauge one from the Great Northern.

D

They were then forced to hire one from the Swilly at a cost of 10s per day, a practice that must have been a little galling.

Disagreements even more profound than those of 1884-5 were brewing between the two parties during the spring of 1887. Some of the trouble stemmed from the railway's claim to the ownership of the strip of land between the river and the road from Pennyburn to the Rock Mill. The claim was strenuously opposed by the Harbour Commissioners, who publicised their grounds of disagreement in a newspaper statement, claiming that it was entirely false and engineered by certain of the Swilly's directors. Then, on 28 June 1887, the Harbour Commissioners gave the Lough Swilly Railway Company formal notice that from 1 January 1888 they were terminating the arrangement for bringing railway traffic into the Middle Quay.

During the second half of 1887, the Swilly made vigorous attempts to argue or to buy the Harbour Commissioners out of their decision, but there the matter rested, and no further passenger trains came beyond the Graving Dock. Some months later (2 June 1888), when all hopes of reconciliation were gone, an aggrieved letter from Dawson, the secretary to the L & LS appeared in the *Londonderry Sentinel*, and from the railway's point of view it provides a summary of the history of the feud.

In June 1885, the Harbour Board made an arrangement with the Railway Company to haul their traffic to and from the Middle Quay and gave them the necessary accommodation to carry on the traffic for the yearly payment of £800. This arrangement was duly carried out until June 1887, when in making arrangements for the summer traffic, it was found necessary to divide the early train and an extra train at 4.0 p.m. The Commissioners, for these additional trains, demanded an increased payment, and on the Company drawing their attention to the fact that their agreement included the haulage of the entire traffic, the Harbour Commissioners at once served a six months notice terminating the agreement on 31 December 1887. . .

When my Directors approached the Harbour Commissioners with a view to ascertaining what new tariff they required, they were met in a most extraordinary manner. They were told that unless they gave up a strip of land and abandoned all claims in connection with it, no agreement could be discussed with them, but that if they conceded this the Commissioners would deal liberally with them. After considerable trouble and counsel's opinion being taken by the directors on the land claims, their opinion being favourable to the company's rights, it was decided by the directors that for the sake of peace and with a view to meeting the request, or rather the demand of the Commissioners, all claim to the land should be withdrawn. This being done my directors waited on the Commissioners on 7th ult. for the purpose of arranging the traffic agreement but to their surprise they were again blocked by the Commissioners demanding the most extraordinary guarantees, which guarantees must be given before they would name the sum to be charged for working the company's traffic over the tramway or discuss the terms. The first guarantee required was an undertaking, binding the shareholders personally not to apply at any future date for an Act of Parliament to extend the Railway nearer Derry.

The second guarantee was to make my Directors personally liable for any accident occurring on the tramway notwithstanding that they had no control over the regulations under which it was worked or the harbour officials carrying on the traffic. My directors asked for the full text of these astounding guarantees, demanded for the first time, with a view to ascertaining their extent and force, and if necessary submitting them to the shareholders, and at the same time requested that the time of notice might be extended to complete the regulations, but the Harbour Commissioners, as will be seen . . . have not supplied the information and whilst the negotiations are in progress sweep the rolling stock off the tramway and lift the rails at the Graving Dock.

I am, dear Sir, yours truly,

Frederick Dawson, Secretary.

It is interesting to reflect that the practice of running passenger trains over the tramway was illegal throughout the whole 19 years. The Lough Swilly Company possessed no powers to run trains beyond the Graving Dock, neither did the Harbour Commissioners have powers to admit or to work passenger-carrying vehicles on their own lines.

THE CITY OF DERRY TRAMWAYS

When the illegal practice ceased, passengers had to make their own way from Graving Dock station into town or to the other two railway stations. An extension of the railway proper into the city centre would have been impossibly expensive.

On 3 September 1892 the City of Derry Tramways Company Ltd was formed to build a tramway along Strand Road, and an Order was granted at Dublin Castle on 30 March 1893. The line, on a gauge of 4 ft 8½ in., extended from the Swilly's Graving Dock station to Shipquay Place, and it was opened in April 1897. A further Order was obtained in August 1897, permitting the line to be extended south to the north-west end of Carlisle Bridge, via Foyle Street and John Street. This extension was built in the autumn of 1897, inspected for the Board of Trade by Lt.-Col. Addison, and opened in December 1897.

There appears to have been no intention to create a tramway system serving the whole of Derry, and bearing in mind the hilly character of much of the city, this is not surprising. The Orders specifically forbade steam haulage, and although electric traction was not precluded, horse traction was always used. Grooved steel rails, weighing 90 lb. per yd, were used and the rolling stock consisted of nine double-deck, open-top vehicles. When the line was first opened only two tramcars had been delivered, but as Col. Marindin, the Inspecting Officer, remarked 'it might be opened at once as two cars will be sufficient at first'. The tramway was virtually owned by Messrs McCrea & McFarland, who also built it. It ceased working in February 1919, having succumbed to competition from motor vehicles.

CHAPTER VI

Expansionist Ideas

THE UNTAPPED NORTH-WEST

While the bifurcating line of railway over which the Swilly worked terminated at Letterkenny and Buncrana, it left much of north-west Donegal untapped. The perennial near-insolvency of the Company during their first 20 years prevented large-scale extensions. By 1885, too, there was no illusion that a gold mine awaited railway promoters. The majority of the people had no great need to travel, except to Fairs or Markets, and had a strictly limited purchasing power. The risk was too great for private enterprise.

But by the 1880s the Government was at last turning a benevolent if belated eye on ways and means of relieving poverty and distress in the poorer parts of Ireland. This eventually took the form of grants to aid the construction of harbours, the purchase of fishing boats and the construction of railways. In 1883 Parliament passed The Tramways & Public Companies (Ireland) Act which triggered off the first attempt at subsidised railway expansion. State assistance became available to tramways, in the form of a guarantee to the Baronies (sub-divisions of counties now disused), and the Treasury was able to repay the Barony half of what it might have paid under the guarantee, provided that this was not more than 2 per cent of the capital, and the line was actually constructed and working. The onus was still on private enterprise.

The Swilly Company were not long in attempting to take advantage of the Act. In 1884 a scheme was publicised for the Buncrana & Carndonagh Light Railway, and in 1885 a proposal for a tramway between Letterkenny and Dunfanaghy. Neither scheme directly emanated from the L & LS, but there is no doubt that public interest and support was largely whipped up by the efforts of the directorate.

The Buncrana & Carndonagh Light Railway seems to have been renamed within a year. On 10 January 1885 the *Londonderry Sentinel* mentioned the Carndonagh & Buncrana Light Railway and gave its readers the estimate of the promoters as £81,000. The application for assistance was put forward, the Irish Board of Works sent their engineer to survey and cost, and an estimate of £110,000 was reached. When it was submitted for Government approval, the Lord Chancellor remarked that a proper estimate should have been prepared in the first place; the application was rejected and the promoters were told to apply again after reconsideration. For the time being, that was the end of the Carndonagh Extension. The 1883 Act was however responsible for the birth of no less than seven Irish narrow-gauge lines, noteworthy being the Druminnin to Donegal extension of the West Donegal Railway.

The tramway proposed between Letterkenny and Dunfanaghy would have linked up the succession of villages of the west side of Lough Swilly and its neighbour inlet, Sheep Haven. The minutes of the L & LS Board first mention the scheme on 22 January 1885, and on 10 February state that J. T. Coddington, C.E., had been 'appointed to make the necessary enquiry concerning the merits of the Letterkenny & Dunfanaghy Tramway . . . as defined upon the plans lodged at this office and with the Secretary of the Grand Jury' of the County of Donegal. (The Grand Juries were the predecessors of the more democratic County Councils.) Once again the scheme languished.

THE ALLPORT COMMISSION

Two years after the passing of the 1883 Act, a Royal Commission on Irish Public Works was appointed. This was presided over by Sir James J. Allport and among various other matters considered was whether the efficiency of the railways as a whole would be improved by changes in their organization and management, and also whether financial help for them ought to be continued along the lines of the 1883 Act. The Allport Commission reported critically in January 1888. Had their findings not been influenced by political considerations, there is little doubt that they would have recommended nationalisation.

The Commission advocated the construction of eleven 'light railways', including two in Donegal. The first was to be from Letterkenny to Falcarragh *via* Kilmacrenan, Creeslough and Dunfanaghy; the second from Stranorlar to Killybegs *via* Glenties and Ardara.

Largely because of the recommendations of the Allport Commission, Parliament passed the Light Railways (Ireland) Act in 1889. This fostered 12 light railway projects, on both the standard gauge of 5 ft 3 in. and on the narrow gauge, most of them in the West of

Ireland. County Donegal benefited by acquiring an extension of the West Donegal from Donegal town to the port of Killybegs, and also a branch from the Finn Valley Railway between Stranorlar and the market town of Glenties. Although the Lough Swilly shareholders authorised their Board to apply again for the Buncrana—Carndonagh line, not for another six years was any positive action taken.

THE CONGESTED DISTRICTS

The chronic poverty of much of the west of Ireland gave the Government ever greater cause for concern, and in 1891 the Congested Districts Board was formed. A district was termed 'congested' where the average rateable value per head of the population was under 30s. Large areas west of a line joining Londonderry city in the north with Bantry in the south were included, the major part of County Donegal thus qualifying. The population was 'congested' not through density of persons to the square mile, but as regards the insufficiency of good land for their support. A contemporary Government report stated:

> In the Congested Districts there are two classes, namely the poor and the destitute. There are hardly any resident gentry; there are a few traders and officials; but nearly all the inhabitants are either poor or on the verge of poverty. . . . The people are very helpful to one another, the poor mainly support the destitute.

The yearly income of a family 'in comparatively good circumstances' was calculated to be around £40, perhaps a quarter of that being migratory earnings of the men as agricultural labourers in Scotland or England. A family in very poor circumstances might annually earn £9 to £10, and a 'good many of the people were little more than free from the dread of hunger, even in a good year'.

With all of central or west Donegal a 'congested district' it is small wonder that the Lough Swilly Railway were in no haste to find capital to extend their railway westward. A more uncertain and unpromising district for railway development would have been difficult to find. Yet it appeared to all that one of the measures that would relieve the situation on a long-term basis was the provision of good rail transport.

The Congested Districts Board began a series of measures aimed at improving the standard of living of the people. Land purchase from the landlords was followed by the sale of enlarged and re-

planned holdings to the tenants on deferred terms. Advice was given
on improved farming methods, livestock breeding and poultry and
egg production. On the coast, expansion of the fishing industry was
encouraged by the provision of larger boats, slipways and improved
landing facilities. Great Britain formed a large potential market for
the fish, but to get them there rapidly from Donegal was next to
impossible. To improve matters, the last of the three pieces of
railway legislation went on the Statute Books as the Railways
(Ireland) Act, 1896.

THE CARNDONAGH AND BURTONPORT EXTENSIONS

The Lough Swilly Company now saw their hopes of the last 15
years move towards realisation. Though they had no intention of
trying to raise capital themselves, they were prepared to work a
line into the unremunerative west, or into Inishowen, provided that
public money put it there. Applications were again made, delibera-
tions ensued and in due course authority was given for two long
extension lines : the Carndonagh Extension and the Letterkenny &
Burtonport Extension.

The geography of the Inishowen peninsula largely determined
the course of the line to Carndonagh. From the old Swilly terminus
at Buncrana, the new route struck NNW along a well-defined valley,
and then turned east towards its goal, 18½ miles from Buncrana.
The line was constructed with a free grant of £98,527 and the
rolling stock was supplied by the Lough Swilly Company at a cost
to them of £11,297.

Thanks to the Congested Districts Board, Burtonport had an excellent harbour. A railway was imperative to make full use of it.
The earlier schemes which envisaged an extension ending at Falcarragh or at Dunfanaghy were thus abandoned. The Burtonport
Extension was less rigidly defined by geography than the Carndonagh one. As the crow flies, the distance from Letterkenny to
Burtonport is 28 miles, but a straight course would have had to
contend with an impassable mountain barrier, trenched by valleys
which ran in quite the wrong direction.

The claims of the coastal villages along the west side of Lough
Swilly and Sheep Haven, canvassed in connection with the 1885
proposals, now had only secondary importance in the views of
officialdom. Burtonport and its fisheries were the target.

The Burtonport Extension line was planned jointly by the Board
of Works and the Londonderry & Lough Swilly Railway Company,

though since the former paid the piper, they determined the tune. On its way to the west, it adroitly avoided both the mountain group and the villages, thereby saving perhaps five miles, but passing close to only one sizeable place, Creeslough. Kilmacrenan, Dunfanaghy, Falcarragh, Crolly and Dungloe had to be content with stations three or four miles away.

During 1898 the Board of Works were closely studying the civil engineering specifications of both the extension lines, to see what economies they could make on the Swilly's proposals. At the half-yearly meeting on 22 August, John McFarland complained of the delays in getting started, and of the irritation that the cheeseparing tactics of the Government were causing.

The Board of Works engineer, W. Batchen, attended a meeting of the Swilly directors on 5 September 1898 and proposed various reductions in the accommodation specifications for the Carndonagh Extension : no goods stores were to be built at Ballymagan, Drumfries or Ballyliffin, while at Clonmany the goods store was not to hold wagons under cover. The sidings at Clonmany were to be shortened by 243 yd, or over 50 per cent, and the goods shed was to be 40 ft by 20 ft instead of the proposed 84 ft by 30 ft. This was followed in February 1899 by a catalogue of minor changes to the specification of the houses, saving a total of £1,883. These economies included leaving off the door knockers (£4), window sills of concrete instead of cut stone (£23-17s) and lighter glass in the windows (£8-6s-8d). The largest item was the use of lime mortar in place of cement, which saved £486.

The contracts for the construction of both extension lines were given to Pauling & Co. Ltd, of Westminster, who shipped over two Kerr, Stuart 0—4—0 saddle-tank engines (maker's nos. 659 and 660) in July 1899 to help in the ballasting. During 1900, Paulings ran short of ballast wagons and the Swilly handed over six of their low-sided flats, later replaced by six new flats from the Lancaster Wagon Co.

The construction of the extension lines involved a good deal of cutting through rock, much of it blasted through hard granite and gritstone. Out on parts of the Burtonport Extension the line traversed waterlogged peat bogs and much trouble was experienced in getting sound foundations for the permanent way. That much of the work could have been better done is clear from certain reports of the engineers in later years. Thus the Swilly's engineer, R. B Newell, wrote to Hunt, the general manager, after a derailment at Crolly in February 1923.

The railway is, as you know, on a very peculiar foundation, partly granite and partly bog. On several occasions when I have been in similar places and noticed a train going past, especially with one of the big engines, I have noticed a complete depression in the railway under the wheels of the engine. This depression, of course, travels with the engine. I have also felt at a distance of 40 feet the ground vibrating strongly.

SHORT OF LOCOMOTIVE POWER

On 7 March 1898, F. G. Miller, the locomotive superintendent, reported on the six engines of the L & LS. Only Nos. 1 and 2 were in good running order. No. 3 was waiting for wheels, and the boiler of No. 4 was away for repairs. Of the two ex-Glenariff engines, No. 5 was 'not safe to run and should not be used again', while No. 6 'will not run through the summer and is not worth repairing'. Along with this sorry tale of neglect, Miller put in a plea for an increase in his pay, then 50s a week, and won a rise of 5s.

Further engines were needed urgently, both to replace the run-down stock, and to work the proposed extension lines. Miller was asked to write to Bowman Malcolm, his opposite number on the Belfast & Northern Counties, for specifications of their narrow-gauge locomotives 'and the names of the best makers', and to approach similarly Mr Livesey on the Donegal Railway. A week later the directors asked him to draw up a specification for one engine for the Lough Swilly line and two for the Carndonagh line. During the ensuing months, the proposal was trimmed from three engines to two, which came in the following year from Hudswell, Clarke of Leeds. In August, Miller was asked to advise the Board on the best length for the Burtonport carriages.

By the time the two Hudswell, Clarke engines arrived, delays to trains were becoming increasingly frequent on the Letterkenny section, due to the poor state of both the engines and the track. The sight of the two new engines was cheering and the Company promptly put them to good use in improving the running to Letterkenny during the month of November. The Board of Works objected to this, and on 1 December the Company learnt that their tormentors were to take legal proceedings to restrain them from using the stock bought for the Carndonagh Extension. Miller must have found this too much, for in April 1900 he resigned and left. As another locomotive superintendent could not be found quickly, the foreman-fitter James Stewart acted as superintendent for eight weeks until John Fisher was appointed. At their meeting on 1 October the Swilly directors ordered that a gratuity of £3 was to be given to Stewart for the extra responsibilities he had shouldered during the interregnum. In a further burst of generosity, it was decided at the same meeting to bring up the wages of Lizzie Harkin, the Gallagh Road agent, to 8s for a week of seven days.

Newly arrived, and with the opening to Carndonagh imminent, Fisher looked his engines over and reported in January 1901. He pointed out that the resources of the Pennyburn shops were limited and suggested that work on the *Donegal* engine (No. 3) might be farmed out to the Belfast & Northern Counties works. Although the B & NC had experience of narrow-gauge engines, and could have loaded the engine at Derry, they declined to assist. The idea of an approach to the Donegal Company at Stranorlar does not appear to have been considered.

By 6 February 1901 Fisher was able to submit a more detailed story—a gloomy one. *J. T. Macky* (No. 1) badly needed new crank-pins and new liners to the eccentrics, although the boiler was satisfactory. *Londonderry* (No. 2) was in the shops and under repair and was expected to be ready in two or three weeks. *Donegal* was in poor order, its axle boxes worn out and the crank pins in need of renewal. The fourth of the old engines, *Innishowen*, was in need of new tyres, crank-pins and side rod brasses. There remained the two new, and unnamed, Hudswell engines of whose use the Board of Works had complained: after a year the wheels of both wanted turning up, and copper stays were needed in the sides of the fire-boxes.

It was nothing new to have the resources of the Swilly's work-shops strained. During the rest of 1901, No. 2 misbehaved conspicuously; she ran off the road at Trady in March, though that was no wonder considering the shaky state of the Letterkenny road, still laid with 40 lb. rails. Then on 17 August she broke down when hauling the 7.30 a.m. ex-Carndonagh, with a fractured steam pipe, and repeated the failure on the Letterkenny line on 6 September.

ECONOMY AND DISAGREEMENT

In the midst of the vicissitudes, the Carndonagh line was opened on 1 July 1901, with three trains in each direction on weekdays and two on Sundays. Abiding by the wishes of the Board of Works, whose tidy mind could only see that engines for the Carndonagh line should be used there and nowhere else, the Swilly saw that the two Hudswell engines worked the first up and down trains. The Dublin photographer, W. Lawrence, was at the terminus to record their arrival and departure. His photograph (see plate 24) shows merely a small knot of interested bystanders and no opening ceremony is on record. Noteworthy in Lawrence's views are the remarkably frail-looking buffers, though they were standard narrowgauge in type, the sparkling clean ballast, and the disciplined spectators watching the arrival from behind the wooden fence. In another, an engine is linked to a pulsometer, lifting water from a lineside well to the station tank.

Work on the Burtonport Extension progressed much less smoothly than did the Carndonagh. Relations between the Company and the Board of Works became more strained. The construction by Pauling was under the supervision of W. Batchen, the Board of Works engineer, and although the L & LS were eventually to work and maintain the line, they had no resident engineer to look after their interests. This in particular was a rankling irritation to John McFarland, and he referred to it frequently.

When the Board of Works submitted plans and specifications of the engines, carriages and wagons for the Burtonport line, the Swilly promptly objected that they were inadequate. In particular, they pointed out that the tank engines proposed were not powerful enough for economic working of mixed trains on the route of 50 miles with heavy gradients and only two passing places. The Board of Works advisers disagreed and the proposed engines and rolling stock were accordingly provided. The engines in themselves were excellent machines, 4—6—0 tanks by Andrew Barclay of Kilmarnock, but limited both in water capacity and power.

On 24 February 1903, Major Pringle inspected the Burtonport Extension on behalf of the Board of Trade. At the same time he took the opportunity to comment adversely on the Graving Dock station, and on the Company's continued use of steam locomotives across the Pennyburn level crossing, two matters about which the Swilly were touchy, to say the least. Major Pringle was satisfied with what he saw between Letterkenny and Burtonport, and the line was opened on 9 March 1903.

From the outset, the working of the Burtonport Extension gave rise to criticism. Initially there were two trains each way on weekdays, and one on Sundays. Within three months, a question was asked in the House of Commons regarding the safety of the methods used by the Swilly, it being claimed that on one occasion (no doubt an excursion, when there would have not been enough carriages) over 100 passengers were conveyed in open wagons and in the guard's and luggage vans.

CHAPTER VII

Working North and West

BAD TIMEKEEPING

At the half-yearly meeting on 31 August 1903, John McFarland enumerated the reasons for the acknowledged bad working of the Burtonport line. His chief complaint concerned the four Barclay locomotives. While in themselves as good as any engines the Company had used, they were unsuited to the line. Their water capacity was only 750 gallons; not only was watering necessary on the 50-mile run west of Letterkenny, but it took 15 minutes instead of four because of the small diameter of the supply pipes. The coal capacity was only 1¼ tons and intermediate coaling was also sometimes needed. It was stated that in 1901 the Swilly's locomotive superintendent and Bowman Malcolm of the B & NC had together recommended that tender engines were best suited to the line.

In a public letter, addressed to the Board of Works, the Swilly complained:

Twelve carriages have been supplied. These would only be sufficient to make up the three trains run, and would necessitate the changing of all passengers at Letterkenny station. It is only by supplementing this supply with our own carriages that all passengers can be run through without being disturbed, or any sufficient provision made for special excursion and such like trains. . . . 60 wagons were supplied, with one horse box and one timber truck. . . . By taking any three consecutive days it will be found that in that period from 60 to 85 wagons pass Letterkenny station on to the Extension. That is, if my company did not make good the deficiency, by providing their own wagons, in three or sometimes two days, the entire new stock would be exhausted and the traffic would have to wait until the wagons had been unloaded. . . . Notwithstanding this your Board have raised objections in your letters to Burtonport wagons being loaded with traffic from Letterkenny to Derry. It evidently being the opinion of your experts that the interchange should be altogether one-sided, or that more delays should be incurred by sentimental shunting of Burtonport wagons (while the supply lasted) for Burtonport goods, and Lough Swilly wagons only for Lough Swilly goods.

The Board of Works had already taken steps to obtain expert advice, but for some reason turned to a comparatively junior person, Basil Hope, the assistant locomotive superintendent of the Midland Great Western. The Swilly secretary wrote referring to a recommendation by Hope that coal should be kept in bags at intermediate stations and served out to the engines on the way :

> In view of these facts, is it any wonder that this company have frequently had to run a wagon of locomotive coal on the trains to replenish the engines en route, and that the disgraceful scenes described in the press of carrying this coal to the engines and bucketing water from streams adjoining the railway have taken place on the Burtonport line.

By the middle of 1903 the Company were in control of 12 engines, but the workshop facilities in Derry remained inadequate. Burtonport, out on a 74-mile limb from Derry, had no repair facilities to speak of, though a fitter was stationed there for a time. Anything seriously wrong with an engine at Burtonport involved either a lengthy limp back to base, or a tow. Fisher, the superintendent, received a reprimand from his directors in April 1904, for his inadequate handling of a situation that was scarcely of his own making.

The minutes for August 1904 contain a list of how engines had caused delays to the Burtonport trains : 30 July, water short in engine; 7 August, engine running hot; 9 August, burst vacuum pipe; 17 August, lead plug fused; 18 August, tube burst; 22 and 23 August, engine running hot. While some of this trouble was due to the stupidity of crews, much of it stemmed from inadequate workshops for which the board of directors refused to vote the necessary money.

In November 1904, Fisher was demoted, and was sent for his sins to Letterkenny as the branch working foreman. Later he went to the Tralee & Dingle Railway, to continue his association with the narrow gauge as far away as he could get in Ireland from his former employers.

TATLOW LOOKS IN

Continued complaints caused the Board of Works in 1905 to institute the first of two formal inquiries into the way in which the Burtonport Extension was being worked. They charged Joseph Tatlow with the task. Tatlow had been born in Sheffield in 1851 and started his career with the Midland Railway of England. After transferring to the Glasgow & South Western, he came to Ireland in 1885, as general manager of the Belfast & County Down. In December 1890 he moved from Belfast to Dublin to become the manager of the Midland Great Western. A brilliant administrator, he came to be in considerable demand on various advisory bodies and commissions, and had in fact taken part in the initial enquiries in 1897 concerning the Carndonagh and Burtonport lines, on behalf of the Irish Board of Works. Strangely his investigation passed unrecorded in the Swilly's minutes.

The situation created by the malfunctioning of the Burtonport line was now exciting widespread comment, and both parties seem to have felt that they were being held to public ridicule by the other. On 3 November 1905 the quarterly meeting of the Londonderry Chamber of Commerce heard a letter from Lord Leitrim, complaining of the state of the line. After discussion, it was formally resolved:

> That in view of the unsatisfactory working of the Burtonport line, which is causing much loss and inconvenience to the interests represented by this Chamber, and in view of the allegation of the Londonderry and Lough Swilly Railway that this unsatisfactory working is due to the defective construction and inadequate and unsuitable equipment of the line, we hereby urge upon the Lords Commissioners of His Majesty's Treasury, the Chief Secretary for Ireland, and the Board of Trade, the necessity for an immediate enquiry into the manner in which the Burtonport line was constructed and equipped by the Board of Works and worked by the Londonderry and Lough Swilly Railway Company.

THE SCOTTER AWARD

Under the agreement between the Swilly Company and the Board of Works, the former not only had a duty to develop the traffic potential but to provide the locomotives, rolling stock, sidings and so on required by additional services. The original service of two trains daily each way was soon seen to be inadequate, and was changed to three. The Swilly, however, refused to find the rolling stock, and followed up by making a claim for £78,000 for alleged incompleteness of civil engineering work and equipment initially provided by the Commissioners of Public Works. For their part the Commissioners refused to provide any further equipment, but were willing to recommend the Treasury to do so if the Company would abandon their additional claims.

The controversy had been rumbling on for five weary years

E

when in 1908 it came before the 1906-10 Vice-Regal Commission on Irish Railways and received thorough ventilation. Settlement did not fall within the terms of reference of the Commission, but its chairman, the elderly Sir Charles Scotter, who was also chairman of the London & South Western Railway, offered to mediate. An agreement was reached in June 1909 between the Company, the Commissioners of Public Works and the Treasury. This, the 'Scotter Award', was virtually an admission of earlier parsimony and it provided for eight items:

1 The Board of Works to pay the Lough Swilly Company the whole of the outstanding balance of the expenses properly and necessarily incurred in respect of promotion and engineering and land valuing.
2 The Board of Works to contribute £2,000 towards the cost of erecting a running shed at Letterkenny, for use by Burtonport engines.
3 The Board of Works to pay £7,000 for additional rolling stock.
4 A crossing place and water supply to be provided at Kilmacrenan. The cost, not exceeding £1,500, to be met out of surplus receipts of the Burtonport Railway, in which the Treasury and the Company had an equal interest.
5 Improvements to be made in the sanitation and heating of the stations.
6 Five extra gate lodges to be built.
7 A new station to be built at Meenbanid (the cost of items 5, 6 and 7 to be met in the same way as item 4).
8 All surplus land on the Burtonport and Carndonagh lines to be sold and the proceeds retained by the Board of Works and applied to improvements on the Burtonport Railway when required.

The £7,000 grant (item 3) towards new rolling stock was spent in the following way, the vehicles being put on the line in March-April 1910:

Two engines (Hawthorn, Leslie 4—6—2T)	£4,100
One carriage, two fish vans, 27 wagons	£2,705
Acetylene lighting for carriages	£195

From the date of the Scotter Award, the Commissioners of Public Works assumed, with some justification, that the line was properly equipped. But though they might hope that there would be no grounds for further complaints, the matter was by no means ended. Instead the Commissioners received a succession of unsatisfactory reports from their own engineer, and also from the public. As ever, the chief complaints were traceable to the Company's failure to look after their locomotives.

In the mind of the Commissioners, six engines were allocated to

JANUARY, 1913

UNTIL FURTHER NOTICE.

M'CREA & M'FARLAND, LIMITED.

The Steamers of above Company

CARRYING MAILS.

Are Intended to Sail (unless prevented by unforeseen circumstances) with Passengers, Goods, and Live Stock,

BETWEEN

RAMELTON, RATHMULLAN, PORTSALON,

AND FAHAN.

FAHAN AND RAMELTON SERVICE.

A Steamer will SAIL between FAHAN and RAMELTON and vice-versa DAILY

(Sundays Excepted) with GOODS as the Tides suit, leaving Ramelton about 3 Hours before High Water, Returning from Fahan Same Day after transhipment of Goods.

FAHAN and RATHMULLAN.

	WEEK-DAYS.	SUNDAYS.
FAHAN to RATHMULLAN,	7.10, 10.15 a.m., & 5 15 p.m.	CANCELLED.
RATHMULLAN TO FAHAN,	8.5 a.m., 12.0 p.m & 6.10 p.m.	

☞ Perishable Goods and Passengers' Luggage must be alongside 20 Minutes before advertised hour of Sailing. ☜

Fares between Fahan and Rathmullan and Vice Versa—Cabin, Single, 9d ; Return, 1s ; Steerage, Single, 4d ; Return, 8d.

SATURDAY to MONDAY TICKETS are issued from Derry to Rathmullan per 9.35 a.m., & 4.30 p.m. Trains.

FARES :—First Class, 2s 6d ; 2nd Class, 2s ; 3rd Class, 1s 2d (available for Return on Monday following).

FAHAN AND PORTSALON.

On TUESDAYS (weather permitting), a Steamer will sail to PORTSALON in connection with 9.35 a.m. Train from Derry, returning from PORTSALON after Transhipment of Goods about 1 p.m

Goods and Passengers Booked at Through Rates.

FARES.

To or from Derry and Ramelton.			To or from Derry & Rathmullan.			To or from Derry & Portsalon		
	SINGLE.	RETURN.		Single.	Return.		Single.	Return.
1st Class and Cabin,	3/4	5/0	1st Class and Cabin, ...	2/4	3/4	1st Class and Cabin,	3/6	5/0
			2nd Class and Cabin, ...	1/9	2/7			
			3rd Class and Steerage, ...	1/0	1/8			
2nd Class and Cabin,	2/8	4/0	1st Class and Saloon Monthly Ticket, ...	25/0		2nd Class and Cabin,	3/0	4/6
			2nd do. and do. do.	20/0				
3rd Class & Steerage 1/8		2/6	3rd do. and Steerage do.	15/0		3rd Class and Steerage, 1/8		3/0

These Fares do not include the Conveyance of Passengers and their Luggage between the Railway Station and Fahan Pier.

☞ Passengers will please procure their Tickets before going on Board.

Cattle and Live Stock booked at Local and Through Rates are carried solely at Owners' Risk, and must be taken charge of by Drovers from Shipment to destination; and under no circumstances will the Steamboat Company be responsible for losses or damages to such Cattle and Live Stock while in their charge, or in that of the Railway Company, or between them.

The Lough Swilly Steamboat Company will not be responsible for Goods after they are discharged from Steamer. If Warehoused, they are entirely at the Risk and Expense of the Owner.

☞ GOODS AND SHIPPING NOTES will be received to within Half-an-hour of Sailing Time. ☜

Cars leave RAMELTON every Morning (Sundays excepted) in time to catch the 8.5 a.m. Steamer from Rathmullan connecting with 8.50 a.m. train from Fahan to Derry, returning to RAMELTON on arrival of the 5.15 p.m. Steamer from Fahan. For further particulars see Car Owners' Advertisement. The running of the Cars is given for the information of the Public, but the Lough Swilly Steamboat Company will not be responsible for any irregularity or any delay occasioned by the running of said Cars.

LOUGH SWILLY RAILWAY.

WEEK DAYS

Down Trains, connecting with Steamers, leave DERRY at *6.15, 9.35 a.m., & *4.30 p.m.

Up Trains, connecting with Steamers, leave Fahan at 8.50 a.m., 2 25 p.m., & 7.10 p.m.

Down Trains marked thus (*) run to CARNDONAGH.

For further information apply at the Lough Swilly Railway Stations : T. STINSON, Agent, Fahan ; or Booking Clerks at Rathmullan, Ramelton, and Portsalon ; or to

M'CREA & M'FARLAND, LIMITED, Foyle St., Londonderry

work the Burtonport line, though in practice the Swilly used the total engine stock as and when they liked, in spite of the occasional embarrassment of an inspection by the Board of Works engineer. In 1911 it was pointed out that five out of the six Burtonport engines were under or awaiting repair. This the Company knew very well, and had they not been using their own engines as substitutes, Burtonport would have seen very few trains. What seems to have infuriated the Commissioners was that two of the engines had lain unattended for 10 or 12 months. During 1912, four of the Burtonport engines were out of action and although the total fell to three during 1913, it was four again when war broke out in 1914.

This situation, handled by a succession of frantic locomotive superintendents, who were goaded by the management, was clearly the result of the latter's inability to realise that the proper maintenance of a complex and non-standard locomotive stock, hammered daily over a difficult and in places ill-kept road, could only be achieved by having good workshops. Since this would cost money, and since every penny spent had to be accounted for not only to the manager but to the chairman of the Board in person, there was little chance of the situation being rectified.

War conditions speedily aggravated the position. A few hundred yards from the Company's workshops at Pennyburn, the Derry shipyard went on to Admiralty work, and drew away some of the Company's small team of fitters and boilermakers, who could hardly be blamed for following higher wages.

BIG ENGINES AND POOR BALLAST

Well before the outbreak of war, however, the Company had taken the matter of engine power into their own hands. Since 1905 two 4—8—0 tender engines had been at work. With a tank capacity of 1,500 gallons, and room for five tons of coal, they took in their stride working out to the ends of the two extensions, though they needed to be turned at the termini. The eight-coupled arrangement resulted in an axle loading just over $6\frac{1}{2}$ tons, which compared well with the eight tons of the Barclay engines, and the 8 tons 6 cwt of the later 'Scotter' engines.

With their experience of eight-coupled engines in mind, the Company turned in 1912 to the same makers, Hudswell, Clarke of Leeds, and ordered a remarkable pair of tank engines. These had leading and trailing bogies, ostensibly to avoid the need for the turntables, and the wheel arrangement of 4—8—4T, the first and the only time that this was used in the British Isles. Although the total weight of these engines came to 58¾ tons, their 16 wheels kept the maximum axle load down. Both the Swilly and the builders were proud of them—the latter used a photograph to illustrate their catalogue even after both the engines had been scrapped!

The 4—8—4 tanks went straight out on to the difficult Burtonport road. *En route* they had to traverse the Tooban—Letterkenny section, originally the Letterkenny Railway's line, and still laid with the original light rails. A series of derailments occurred through 1909 and 1910, and finally Major Pringle of the Board of Trade recommended that a speed limit of 25 m.p.h. should be imposed until the track could be relaid with something stronger than the old 40 lb. rail, by then so much worn that they were down to 36 lbs. to the yard.

Ballasting was a contributory cause of derailments, and to judge by reports the material seems to have been unwashed gravel. Certainly no specific mention of crushed stone ballast is made before 1915. On 16 September 1911 a rather odd accident at Newmills focussed attention on the poor state of the Burtonport Extension's permanent way. A carriage door or doors appear to have been opened when the train was moving, and they were ripped off by contact with the parapet of an underbridge. The initial move was to fine the driver for failing to stop. That disciplinary matter attended to, Richardson, the engineer, was told to make a general check of parapet clearances on the Burtonport road. He did so, and on 27 November reported that in general open carriage doors were unable to clear the girders of bridges because the track was too low, owing to insufficient ballast. The line was ordered to be raised. Ingham Sutcliffe complained of the 'spongy condition' of the Burtonport line in two places in March 1913, which suggests that even then the ballast was far from what it should have been. But eventually the Letterkenny section was reballasted. A stone quarry was opened in Cloncairney townland, near the Barnes Gap, and a siding laid to bring the ballast out with a rake of 24 wagons.

It almost goes without saying that the railway was reprimanded by the Commissioners of Public Works for purchasing such monsters as the 4—8—4 tanks without consultation, and that once they possessed engines capable of getting to Burtonport unwinded, the railway worked away unheeding.

COMPETITION AT LETTERKENNY

From 1903, Strabane had become a railway crossroad. The narrow-gauge rails of the Donegal Railway came up the Finn Valley from Stranorlar, climbed across the standard-gauge Great Northern, and headed for Derry on the east side of the River Foyle. Twelve miles north-west of Strabane was Letterkenny, and between the two, in the fertile lowland part of the county, were the villages of Raphoe, a diocesan seat, and Convoy with its important woollen mills. The incentive thus offered to railway promoters resulted in the incorporation of the Strabane, Raphoe & Convoy Railway Company in 1903. In the following year authority was given to continue the line to Letterkenny, and the Company's title became the Strabane & Letterkenny Railway.[1]

The Strabane & Letterkenny was partly sponsored by local people, though the Donegal Railway Company were permitted to contribute share capital and were to work and maintain the line. During the period of construction of the S & L, the Donegal Railway Company were purchased by the Midland Railway of England and the Great Northern of Ireland. So from 1 May 1906, administration of the Donegal Railway passed to a board of six members, three from each of the owning companies, and the name of the concern became the County Donegal Railways Joint Committee.

The Swilly opposed the Strabane & Letterkenny, seeing it as a menace to their monopoly of transport in the Lagan, as that part of the county was colloquially termed, but protests were ineffective against the powerful influence of the Midland and the Great Northern. Even the obvious argument that the new construction would irreparably damage the earning capacity of the Letterkenny Railway, mortgaged since 1887 to the Board of Works, failed to stem the tide.

So the Strabane & Letterkenny came over the hill, the line being opened on the 3 ft gauge on 1 January 1909. The black engines brought their trains down the bank from Glenmaquin, and a mile from Letterkenny cheekily leaped over the Swilly's line. The new line then ran a short way north of the Swilly's track and into a terminus immediately alongside the through station at the east end of the town where the Letterkenny Railway ended and the Letterkenny & Burtonport Extension Railway began.

---

[1] See *The County Donegal Railways*, pp. 40-48.

One might well have asked why the two lines could not have shared a station. The only tangible evidence that one line acknowledged the existence of the other was the single connecting spur, built mainly for the transfer of wagons. Even that was inhibited because the CDRJC buffers were three inches above the Swilly's, and the vacuum bags would not join without an adaptor.

Relations at Letterkenny between the two companies were never unstrained, and from time to time one accused the other of attempting to take away their trade. In later years when Hunt was in control at Derry and Forbes at Stranorlar, the two managements encouraged touting for cattle traffic at the Letterkenny Fair.

Londonderry and Lough Swilly Railway.

Letterkenny Hiring Fair,

FRIDAY, 14th MAY, 1915.

On above date the *TRAIN SERVICE* between BURTONPORT and LETTERKENNY will be as under :—

		a.m.	a.m.	a.m.	p.m.			a.m.	p.m.	p.m.	p.m.
LEAVE	BURTONPORT, ...	6.0	8.30	10.40	3.30	LEAVE	LETTERKENNY, ...	9.2	1.30	4.0	6.43
Do.	DUNGLOE ROAD, ...	6.6	8.37	10.46	3.36	Do.	OLD TOWN, ...	9.8	1.36	4.10	6.48
Do.	KINCASSLAGH ROAD,	6.13	8.45	10.53	3.42	Do.	NEW MILLS, ...	c	1.46	4.20	6.53
Do.	CROLLY,	6.33	9.3	11.10	4.0	Do.	FOXHALL, ...	9.26	1.53	4.27	7.4
Do.	GWEEDORE,	6.46	9.20	11.21	4.15	Do.	CHURCHHILL, ...	9.39	2.4	4.38	7.15
Do.	CASHELNAGORE,	7.7	9.39	11.39	4.34	Do.	KILMACRENAN, ...	9.53	2.19	4.50	7.30
Do.	FALCARRAGH,	7.17	9.52	11.49	4.44	Do.	CREESLOUGH, ...	10.22	2.50	5.30	8.0
Do.	DUNFANAGHY ROAD,	7.39	10.16	12.11	5.9	Do.	DUNFANAGHY ROAD,	10.28	2.55	5.35	8.5
Do.	CREESLOUGH,	7.50	10.27	12.22	5.20	Do.	FALCARRAGH, ...	10.53	3.22	5.55	8.29
Do.	KILMACRENAN,	8.16	10.53	12.48	5.47	Do.	CASHELNAGORE, ...	11.6	3.35	6.5	8.41
Do.	CHURCHHILL,	8.26	11.5	12.58	5.58	Do.	GWEEDORE, ...	11.27	4.10	6.29	9.1
Do.	FOXHALL,	8.38	11.17	1.10	6.10	Do.	CROLLY, ...	11.38	4.26	6.45	9.10
Do.	NEWMILLS,	8.43	11.22	1.15	6.15	Do.	KINCASSLAGH ROAD,	11.57	4.41	7.0	9.29
Do.	OLD TOWN,	8.51	11.31	1.23	6.24	Do.	DUNGLOE ROAD, ...	12.4	4.46	7.5	9.35
ARRIVE	LETTERKENNY, ...	8.55	11.34	1.27	6.28	ARRIVE	BURTONPORT, ...	12.10	4.50	7.10	9.40

MARKET TICKETS will be issued to Letterkenny by 6.0 and 8.30 a.m. Ordinary Trains.

Printed at the Londonderry Sentinel Office.—10515

J. L. CLEWES, General Manager.

Handbill of services in connection with a Letterkenny Hiring Fair

Since 1883, the Swilly appear to have had no turntable at Letterkenny. None is shown on early plans of the station, though a Board minute of 20 September 1886 mentions that the engineer was 'to arrange for a wall to be made at Letterkenny turning table'. Its existence or position is uncertain, and certainly its absence would not be critical until the arrival of the 4—8—0 tender engines in 1905. Since the S & L terminated at Letterkenny, they had a turntable from the start. The Swilly pocketed their pride and came to an agreement with the Joint Committee whereby they could turn their engines in the s & l yard, and be charged 6d for the privilege. Eventually the Swilly put a turntable in front of their own engine shed.

Competition of a more serious kind was first noted in the minutes of 1912. A 'Ferguson's steam lorry' was stated to be carrying an estimated 30 tons of goods every week on the road to Buncrana. In the following May, Mr Gallagher of Newtoncunningham bought 'a road motor engine' and began to compete with the Swilly in the Manorcunningham and Newtoncunningham district. But the development of road transport in the Swilly's area was both late and slow; the Belfast & Northern Counties Railway had a steam road wagon for goods in November 1902, and had put on a parcels service by a motor van three years before that.

STAFF

In November 1903 the Company had experienced their first major labour troubles. A demand for higher wages and better working conditions by the Amalgamated Railway Servants Society, which had become established in and around Derry, was rejected. The Company refused to negotiate, a strike was called and dismissals followed, with eviction of linesmen and their families from the railway's cottages.

To replace the dismissed employees, non-union men were engaged. They came mainly from outside Derry, and to house some of them the Company built some substantial wooden huts at Pennyburn. Sixty years later these huts were doing duty as the administrative offices.

With the departure of James Fisher in 1904, there began a turnover of locomotive superintendents which must be unique in railway history. Five came and went between 1904 and 1909. At the end of that year, Charles H. Swinerd took up the position at £4 a week. He seems to have tried to function more adequately than his predecessors, making recommendations for the workshop power plant, visiting the Hawthorn, Leslie works to inspect the two new engines being built to replace the four old Hawthorns, now worn out, and dismissing a fireman for having caused a collision between Nos. 2 and 3 at Letterkenny. Some extension was belatedly made to the workshop accommodation; but soon friction developed with the directors. On 1 June 1910 Swinerd was reprimanded for slowness in getting tyres turned on the wheel lathe, among other items; in October he asked for a tool for boring out cylinders, to be told by John McFarland that such a tool had not been needed for 25 years, a fact promptly challenged by Swinerd, who saw his professional reputation at stake.

Swinerd and his clerk were dismissed over the matter of locomotive coal stocks, and Ingham Sutcliffe became the 13th locomotive superintendent, lasting three years—longer than his six immediate predecessors. The minutes for New Year's Day 1912 record that 'he was told it behoved him to leave nothing undone that he could do, that the Directors would not stand between him and anything necessary to maintain the engines and run them to time, and that if he failed in this, he would be held responsible', with special reference to the Burtonport road. He 'travelled up and down on the engines' to watch fuel consumption, abolished the duplicate numbering of L & LS and L & BE engines—but left in 1914, when the breathless succession of superintendents began again.

Almost as cinematographic as the passage of the locomotive superintendents were the changes in the Company's civil engineers, or permanent-way inspectors as they were named until 1903. After C. E. Stewart left in 1888, the record for longevity was held by James Cairns, in office from 1892 to 1903. From then until 1915 there were four engineers, the last of them responsible for a programme of reballasting the Letterkenny Railway. After the engineer's office had been vacant a month, Sidney F. Jones, assistant engineer to the North Staffordshire Railway, arrived in May 1916. A conscientious man (who also did spells on the County Donegal Railways and the LMS [NCC]), he must have rebelled at the incipient chaos which faced him. He soon left, as did several successors, stability coming in the person of R. B. Newall, who held office from 1916 to 1937.

On the management side, Andrew Spence had been secretary and traffic manager since 1901 (when Frederick Dawson had resigned), and in 1912 was promoted to manager, at the age of 38. He died suddenly two years later at his Derry home, leaving a widow and ten children, and a gap in the staff which was not easily filled. The post of traffic manager went to J. L. Clewes, who had been first with the Midland of England, and then with the Derwent Valley Light Railway at York.

His management lacked vigour, and in September 1916 the chairman imported Henry Hunt from the Great Central to be general manager. Clewes promptly revolted and left. Three months later, the traffic superintendent, John May, also left, refusing to be made Hunt's assistant.

Early in 1914, John McFarland found his public services, including those to the Swilly, suitably recognised by his elevation to the Baronetcy. As Sir John McFarland, Bart, he was presented with a silver tea and coffee service by his shareholders at the February meeting of the railway Company in which he had become such a dominant figure.

Although much was wrong with the line, the market value of Lough Swilly £10 shares had come up from a few shillings to over par under John McFarland's chairmanship. The dividend had grown from nothing to a steady 7 per cent. These were facts which shareholders appreciated, if not the Board of Works. The chairman, incidentally, had acted as engine driver during the strike of 1903. The Press reported that he 'stuck to work from morning until late at night. He had one very narrow escape. Some scoundrel placed two great rocks on the line at Ballymagan and very nearly derailed the train which Mr McFarland was driving.'

Every expenditure had to be justified to the chairman. In April 1910 he explained to his fellow-directors that though there were complaints because the last train from Buncrana had been altered to leave earlier, at 6.25 p.m., this saved money. 'Bringing in the trains in daylight saved the burning of oil,' the secretary minuted. The chairman's interest extended to such details. At each Board meeting he insisted on consideration of the reasons for delays to trains. In February 1912 a practice was started which continued until 1917: every Saturday afternoon the week's accounts and returns of delays were delivered at his home.

There is a brief mention in the minutes of a derailment on the Letterkenny line on 22 May 1912. The reason for it cannot have been the usual one of faulty permanent way, for driver Deeney, junr, and the brakeman were promptly dismissed. Driving was in the Deeneys' blood (this man's father had been handling Swilly engines 30 years earlier) and the driver seems to have been badly missed. A month after the dismissal, the directors were asked that he should be reinstated 'and punished by being permanently transferred to Burtonport'. Shades of Siberia; but the Board were adamant. They must have relented some time later, for J. Deeney, junr, was listed among the Swilly drivers in October 1915, the other nine at that time including J. Deeney, senr, H. Baird, R. Turner, P. Tierney, D. Tully, H. Boyle, R. Quinn, R. McGuinness and H. Quigley.

Minor level-crossing accidents were fairly frequent in the easy-going west, where the gates at unattended crossings were often conveniently left open. In July 1913 Sergt Pat Geehan of the Royal Irish Constabulary decided to make an example of Maggie McGee of Bunbeg. Maggie had failed to shut the gates at an accommodation crossing after she had driven a herd of cattle through, and the sergeant had seen it all. The matter went to the Bunbeg Petty Sessions. The Lough Swilly Railway solicitor said that 'very few who passed through the crossings ever closed the gates behind them', but Maggie's sin of omission cost her a nominal fine.

Some light relief came before the Board in March 1912 in the form of an anonymous letter. The writer, probably feeling that he was handling political dynamite, informed the directors that stationmaster Algeo at Manorcunningham was teaching a band. The members of the Board considered the situation thus presented with due care, and asked the secretary 'to advise Algeo that while there are no objections to him teaching a band in his spare time, he is not to parade the roads with it, especially if it is a party organisation'.

Platform elevation of Carndonagh station

CHAPTER VIII

Tatlow Investigates Again

'A FIT PERSON TO INSPECT . . .'

The Railways (Ireland) Act of 1896 provided that the Board of Works might at any time appoint 'a fit person to inspect and report upon the condition of the undertaking and the working, maintenance and development of the same'. If an adverse report emerged the Privy Council might then make an Order appointing a manager or receiver of the undertaking armed 'with such powers as should be specified in the Order'.

By 1917 the state of the L & BE had exhausted the patience of the Board of Works and on 11 April the chairman asked Joseph Tatlow to make a second enquiry. Tatlow arrived from the Midland Great Western's headquarters in Dublin, investigated immediately, and reported his findings on 7 May 1917 in a remarkable document of 19 pages. The volume is twice that size since it includes a report by the Commissioners of Public Works to the Lord Lieutenant of Ireland, and also two Appendices to Tatlow's text.

He began in Derry itself. Of the Graving Dock Terminus he wrote scathingly:

> The passenger station is a rough, uncouth structure, is not lighted from the roof and the interior is very dark. It is also partially used as a goods store, and is malodorous and unpleasant. On the down passenger platform cattle are regularly unloaded from the trains. The station is calculated to retard rather than to encourage passenger traffic, particularly pleasure, excursion and tourist traffic, and therefore adversely affects the Burtonport railway. The goods store is too small, the siding accommodation insufficient, and much difficulty in working is experienced.

Crossing the road to Pennyburn he noted that:

> The locomotive and carriage and wagon workshops are good buildings, constructed a few years ago, and to the cost of which I under-

stand the Government largely contributed; but the engine shed and the carriage shed are old wooden erections, and are both in a deplorably ruinous condition. Some of the Burtonport engines are stabled in the engine shed and some of the Burtonport carriages are accommodated in the carriage shed. Neither shed has any pretension to being weather-proof, but let in the rain freely, and both are in a broken-down state such as absolutely beggars description.

Tatlow spent three days on a close inspection of the Burtonport line, travelling out by car with Henry Hunt, visiting and inspecting each station, and meeting at the same time the merchants and traders in the district. He came back on the engine of a special train, riding with Hunt and R. B. Newall, the civil engineer.

Tatlow gave systematic descriptions of 12 stations on the extension, and although he does not specifically criticise the Board of Works' design, the mere fact that on six occasions the crude or inadequate toilet facilities receive adverse comment emphasises the result of the Board's cheeseparing tactics. Though Tatlow did not intend it to be, the report is largely a condemnation of the planners rather than of the operators. Thus of Gweedore:

> This station, being in the centre of an important tourist district and having adjacent a well-known hotel, frequented by a good class of tourists, would by any self-respecting railway company, be kept in a clean, tidy and, as far as possible, attractive condition. I am sorry to say that the reverse is the case; it is dirty, slovenly, untidy and very deficient of paint. The ladies' waiting room is a disgrace. It has a concrete floor, which looks rude and uncouth. Gweedore is a well-enough constructed station, and with ordinary care and attention, could be kept quite attractive looking. The palings of the station are in bad order. The stationmaster's office is on a lowel level than the platform, and his access to the latter is round-about and awkward. The construction of a few steps to the platform would save him time and labour, and be a great convenience. The signal frame is on the platform, and uncovered and frequently unworkable from frost or snow. It should be covered for protection and locked against interference except when in use.

Tatlow wrote of 'the deplorably inefficient condition of the engines'. He referred to the six Burtonport engines, only two of which (Nos. 2 and 4) were capable of working at the time of his visit. The two 4—8—4 tank engines were not in use: No. 5 had been in the shops since 14 September 1916, and No. 6 was across at Stranorlar for heavy repairs at the CDRJC's shops, by order of the Irish Railways Executive Committee. It was no wonder that some of the Swilly's own engines were used to work trains to Burtonport, a mortal sin in the eyes of the Commissioners of Public Works.

Tatlow gave a table of these iniquities:

	Year 1916			1917 (to 21 April)
No.	Days used		No.	Days used
11	...	19	7	...	18
12	...	43	13	...	97
13	...	98	15	...	33
14	...	268		

The lack of engine-repair facilities anywhere on the Burtonport line is mentioned, and must again be taken as criticism of the Government planners, who failed to provide a fitter's shop to maintain the engines which they insisted must work in isolation.

Ernest Maslin came in for close examination, but he passed muster:

> I questioned the Locomotive Superintendent as to how he accounted for the engines being in such a deplorable condition. He said he was satisfied that it could only be caused by serious neglect in the past in maintenance and repairs, to the employment of an incompetent mechanical staff, and to careless and inefficient drivers. With this I thoroughly agree. He stated that when he took up duty in April 1915, he discovered that he would have great trouble owing to the dissatisfied condition of his men, that the Directors interfered too much, and that he was not allowed proper control; that in the first twelve months there were continual disputes and stoppages, and that for a considerable part of this time they were without the services of fitters and boilermakers. He said there was no fitter or mechanical man stationed at the Burtonport end of the line, and that running repairs had to be performed by the Londonderry staff, which caused loss of time and unnecessary labour. He addressed various communications to the then General Manager regarding the conditions of affairs and complained that the men were underpaid and that he was unable to get good men in consequence; he also complained that the men were not all treated fairly, in regard to hours of duty and wages, and that the hours were in many instances excessive.

The report goes on to detail the long hours worked by the drivers, occasionally 20 or 21 hours per day, and usually about 14 hours. Mention is made of the practice of transferring men to the employment of Messrs McCrea & McFarland from time to time, either in connection with their Lough Swilly steamers, their Derry tramway, their carting department, or to the chairman of the Company for work on house property, etc. That this was done is not really surprising in view of the inter-relationship of the firm with the Lough Swilly Railway Company as its cartage and steamboat agents, but it irritated Tatlow, and he condemned it.

The late running of trains during 1917 was investigated next, and has background interest. During January the up trains were over four hours late on two occasions. Of 432 trains only seven reached their destination on time.

The electric train staff instruments came in for caustic comment:

> The condition of the Electric Train Staff instruments is serious. They are and have been for a long time in a useless state, rendering the Train Staff system incapable of being carried out. The General Manager, Mr. Hunt, informs me that the first intimation he received of anything being seriously wrong was in a letter he received from your Secretary[1] on 2nd January last, and that the Engineer had not previously reported the matter to him, but it is right to say that the present Engineer only came into the Company's service in November last and had a good deal to look after.
>
> At KILMACRENAN I found that the staff for the Letterkenny section was not working, nor had it been for the week previous. The instrument for the section to Creeslough has been unworkable for the past two weeks.
> At CREESLOUGH the staff to Letterkenny is out of order and unworkable for the past three or four months and is still in that condition. The staff to Gweedore is not in use and has been so for the past three weeks.
> At GWEEDORE the staff is not working and has been in that condition since the station-master came there in December last.
> At BURTONPORT the staff has been out of order and unworkable since last September.

The failure of carriage lighting was a subject of public criticism. The Company admits its failure and that the trains were frequently run without any light whatever in the carriages. There was also a paragraph on the staffing of the stations:

> The stationmasters at the several stations seem, on the whole, to be capable and industrious men, but the number . . . of porters is very scanty, and frequently stationmasters have to call in help from the permanent-way department. As the labour of the permanent-way department men is urgently required on the line, it is most undesirable to take any of them away, except for emergencies. I also find that they are often removed from their duty in connection with the loading of locomotive coal. This is open to the same objection.

Thus did Tatlow majestically sweep aside the Swilly's economical use of their small labour force. He ended his remarkable indictment of the Swilly directorate and management with a 'Conclusion' of which this is the leading paragraph:

> It is clear that the Burtonport line is not in good condition and is not, and has not been, efficiently worked, maintained, or developed.

[1] i.e., of the Commissioners of Public Works.

Everything has, for years past, been allowed to run down: the direction and management have been characterised by extreme parsimony; and the disabled condition of the engines is undoubtedly due to the lack of proper upkeep which must have been going on for years. The state of the permanent way shews a want of proper maintenance; and the condition of the stations, buildings, and of the carriages, all speak of neglect.

THE CHAIRMAN RESIGNS

The Tatlow Report burst on the shareholders and the public alike with a thunderous roar. No railway company in Ireland had ever suffered the indignity of a study such as Tatlow had made, and no chairman had to face such public criticism. The 20-year-old feud had come to its climax, and the Board of Works had won.

The position of the chairman became untenable, and on 23 May he resigned. On 30 May at the Council Chamber, Dublin Castle, the report and its implications were considered by a Judicial Committee of the Privy Council. As a result, a 'manager or receiver of the undertaking' was appointed for a term of two years—no less a person than Henry Hunt—and the Company were ordered to put £10,000 at his disposal to enable the line to be properly repaired.

Henry Hunt, who had been installed by Sir John McFarland some eight months earlier, had in fact been to a great extent instrumental in unseating the man who had brought him to Derry. It is apparent from the report that Tatlow found Hunt most co-operative during the investigation and he was referred to as 'a good railway man, capable and experienced . . . he has assumed, and exercises, an authority which none of his predecessors possessed, and is keen to do all he can to improve matters and develop the railway'.

It is probable that Hunt came to Derry knowing comparatively little of how the railway was being run. He soon found that the management was largely in the hands of Sir John, and the salaried officials were dominated by his striking personality and his remarkable business ability. It must have become apparent that serious trouble was brewing over the running of the Burtonport Extension, and that the long-drawn tussle between Sir John McFarland and the Board of Works was bound, sooner or later, to result in a showdown. He found that some directors themselves were critical of their chairman's policies, and Brice Mullin in particular was ready to step into the chair if opportunity arose.

From many aspects, the withdrawal of Sir John from the arena was a tragic conclusion to his long association with the Swilly.

When he joined the Board in 1884 the Company was bankrupt, and he was mainly instrumental in bringing it to solvency. He did that in the only way possible, by the exercise of economy in all things save personal energy. Armed with the Tatlow Report, his critics conveniently forgot his many years of untiring effort; the Scotter Award's vindication of his early criticism of the ill-equipped extension went for nothing, as did the little Company's magnificent shouldering of the extraordinary burden of heavy naval and military traffic from the outbreak of the war, when three large military camps, two forts and a naval base were situated on Lough Swilly.

On 11 June 1917 an extraordinary general meeting of the L & LS proprietors was held at Pennyburn. The new chairman, Brice Mullin, spoke in some detail of the penalties which had been imposed by the Government and the reasons behind them. Referring to Sir John McFarland, Mullin said:

> It is not necessary for me to further refer to the past except to say that if my predecessor in office, who unlike myself, can claim to be a railway expert, has made mistakes, it was certainly not due to any want of attention to the duties of his office. On the contrary, he has given the best years of his life to the Company . . . to have brought up the dividends from nothing to seven per cent, and the market value of the £10 shares from a few shillings to over par, is a great achievement, and one which the shareholders should be grateful for, but if the same objects could have been attained consistent with greater efficiency and development, the shareholders would today have a more valuable asset, the public a better service, and the new Board a much easier task before them.

Platform elevation of Ballymagan station

CHAPTER IX

The Troubled Years

THE FIRST WORLD WAR

In following the events which led to the Tatlow enquiry, little mention has been made of the impact of war, except for the demands of the Derry shipyard on the small local pool of maintenance staff.

The first effect was a decline of the fish traffic along the Burtonport Extension—thousands of tons of fresh and cured herrings, kippers, mackerel, salmon, other white fish and shellfish, railed regularly from Burtonport, Kincasslagh, Gweedore, Falcarragh, Dunfanaghy and Creeslough for the Belfast, Dublin, Scottish and English markets. The Buncrana fish traffic stopped entirely, for Swilly became a naval base. A boom was built across the Lough, which virtually closed it to other shipping. There was, however, the compensation of traffic to and from three large military camps on the east of the Lough, two near Clonmany and one at Buncrana.

Tourist traffic fell away, though the weekend excursion trains from Derry to Fahan and Buncrana continued to be patronised. Operating costs were increased, coal doubling in price during the war, and continuing to rise after it to a 1921 peak, when it cost three times as much as in 1913. Wages were also up. Between 1903 and 1913 those of the locomotive department were reasonably steady at around £1,700 per year. Figures were not published during the war but by 1922 the figure had swelled to £6,800, and in 1924-5 reached £7,900. It took the 'depression years' of the 1930s to drag them down to below £7,000.

The wages paid to the staff of the small narrow gauge Swilly were always lower than those of the Irish main-line companies. This was most felt in Derry, where Swilly, Midland and Great Northern men could meet and swap experiences over a bottle of stout. A strike of Swilly men was called in September 1915 to reinforce the men's demands for a War Bonus of 2s per week. That was the beginning of an inevitable spiral.

The new manager, Henry Hunt, was determined to act as a new broom, though apparently without much long-term idea of where to find the money for sweeping changes. The adverse criticism of the Graving Dock station had been taken to heart, and in spite of the war, in August 1917 a proposal was made to build a new terminus at Pennyburn and abandon the line beyond the Strand. A start was made on setting out the new station on the ground, but nothing much could be done until Parliamentary sanction was obtained. The necessary bill was submitted to Parliament in the spring of 1918. The Derry Corporation arranged to oppose it, and in March 1918 started discussions with the L & LS regarding the building of a road subway at Pennyburn. The Swilly stalled by agreeing to the Corporation's request, provided that the Board of Trade would certify that a subway was necessary. Then on 21 November 1918 the Act was passed. Besides giving powers for a new terminus, it legalised the use of the Pennyburn level crossing. Hardly was the Act passed than unsettled conditions made it inadvisable to build a new station; by the middle 20s it was clear that it would never materialise.

From January 1917 (over two years after a similar move in Great Britain) Irish railways were placed in the hands of a Government committee. Probably the most important aspect of the Irish Railways Executive Committee's jurisdiction as it affected the Swilly was the ordering of the major overhaul of No. 6 locomotive (one of the two 4—8—4 tanks) to be done by the CDRJC at Stranorlar in April 1917. Boiler repair work was also farmed out, No. 1's boiler going to the MGW's shops at Broadstone in Dublin in July 1918. During 1918 a shortage of carriages became manifest on the little Cork, Blackrock & Passage Railway, and the Swilly were ordered to lend five third-class carriages. In exchange four thirds came to the Swilly from the CDRJC.

Tatlow's criticism of the state of the stations was followed during 1917 and 1918 by work on both the Burtonport and Carndonagh line buildings, though the latter can have had little need of it. This work came at a time when the war restrictions were most felt. In July 1917 Maslin wrote: 'We are now debarred from obtaining any imported timber and all timber used in connection with repairs has to be sawn and prepared from the log'.

The succession of locomotive superintendents has already been followed up to the arrival of Ernest Maslin in May 1915. His monthly reports to the manager show an enthusiasm which must at times have been hard to maintain. By July 1918, however, pressure was easing a little: 'I am pleased to report that in the matter of staff we are now in a much better position than we have ever been during my time and I have as many men at present as I can advantageously employ in my shops.' He also mentions the dispatch of the last of the five carriages to the CB & P: 'They were all sent away in good order and in running condition and will not reflect any discredit on the Swilly.'

Three months later Maslin was asked to resign, following an enquiry made by Bowman Malcolm, the locomotive engineer of the Midland (NCC). The terms of reference were set out by Tatlow and were based on Maslin's apparent refusal to give priority to the overhaul of Burtonport engines. Final paragraphs of Maslin's last report, dated 3 October 1918, state: 'I have been engaged, and strenuously engaged at that, in underpinning the foundation upon which to reconstruct the whole. Foundation work is not very showy, and it has required all the level-headedness possible to concentrate the energy of the staff upon the most important matters, which only will make for permanent stability.'

With that, Maslin left Derry. For a time his foreman deputised, then another superintendent came and went. Permanence was at last established when W. Napier came from the Belfast & Co. Down Railway, to hold office for 32 years.

THE UNEASY PEACE

No sooner had the war ended than the task of rehabilitation was frustrated and complicated by the current Irish political situation. It had been evident at least since 1916 that British rule over a unified Ireland was coming to an end, and in July 1921 the island was divided into two self-governing portions under the Irish Treaty. County Donegal was placed in the Irish Free State and County Londonderry in Northern Ireland. The Swilly therefore had their headquarters three miles inside Northern Ireland, but the bulk of their track mileage was in the Irish Free State.

For some time before partition there had been increasing civil disorder. All the Irish railways suffered to some extent, but the Swilly were particularly vulnerable since the Buncrana and Carndonagh lines served British naval facilities and shore batteries. A series of incidents resulted, aimed at making British military occupation impossible. Their crews were threatened with violence or death if they conveyed armed troops, police or material destined for them. From July 1920 many of the staff refused to have anything to do with military trains, or even ordinary trains with a few troops on board, producing the so-called 'Munitions Strike'. Only a few crews were bold enough to continue work in the face of threats. The monthly reports by the locomotive superintendent, Napier, gave an illuminating picture of the difficulties:

July 1920: As you are aware the running during the past fortnight was seriously interfered with, by the refusal of a number of the enginemen and guards to work trains conveying armed troops, and between 17th and 28th inst. as a result of their action in this matter, 8 Drivers and 8 Firemen were suspended.

August 1920: For having worked a train conveying armed troops, Driver Quinn was kidnapped on 1st inst., and released upon giving an undertaking not to do it again.

October 1920: In consequence of the munitions dispute 23 enginemen have been suspended and the foot plate staff has now been reduced to 3 drivers and 3 firemen. In the running dept., 8 engine cleaners, 2 carriage and wagon examiners and 2 labourers have been paid off, their services being no longer required.

November 1920: Owing to the presence of armed troops on the 7.30 a.m. train at Derry on 1st inst., the enginemen refused to work the train, and were, therefore, suspended. 25 enginemen are now under suspension for refusal to work trains conveying armed troops or police, and the staff is now reduced to 2 crews. In consequence of the closing of the Letterkenny, Burtonport and Carndonagh lines, 16 hands in the running department and 19 hands in the shops have been dismissed.

The Burtonport line remained closed for eight weeks, and the Carndonagh line from 7 October until 30 December 1920. The reign of terror continued into 1921 and again Napier's reports summarise the story:

January 1921: As you are aware, engine No. 2B was derailed and sustained serious damage when working a troop train on 12th inst. by running into boulders which had been placed between the rails at 72 mile post on the Burtonport line. Some damage was also caused to cab fittings by rifle fire . . . the cab was suddenly filled with scalding steam, it was pitch dark, and a heavy fire was being directed on the train. The enginemen were Driver Turner and Fireman Crawford. The damage to the engine consisted of one broken eccentric strap, brake work bent and twisted, one driving horn block broken, cab damaged and ash pan destroyed.[1]

[1] This troop train episode was spread over two nights. The troop train left Derry at 2 a.m. on 11 Jan., hauled by No. 2B with Bob Turner driving. No. 13, driven by Hedley Connell, ran in front as a light engine and proceeded through the night with Connell opening the gates and Turner's guard closing them. At Skeoge, near Bridge End, the trip nearly ended when Turner hit No. 13, but did not do much damage to the light engine. They eventually got to Burtonport. On the next night the derailment took place.

February 1921 : On the 7th inst., when working the 2.20 p.m. train ex-Burtonport, engine No. 1B ran into a number of large boulders which had been placed on the line in a cutting at 69½ mile post, resulting in the derailment of the engine and the carriages attached to it. . . . The boulders were wedged underneath the first coach, which was also derailed, and thrown against the side of the cutting. . . . The engine and attached carriage were very seriously damaged, the engine bogie so much so that it had to be removed and sent to Derry in a wagon, the engine being pulled home on its remaining wheels. On 11th inst., engines No. 12S and 13B were also damaged by running into obstructions on the line, near Creeslough and Kincasslagh Road stations respectively, in each case after dark. . . .Four of our best engines are out of commission, three of them indefinitely, and the programme of repair work in the shops has received a serious set-back, which is particularly unfortunate, inasmuch as the arrears of work had been almost overtaken.

In March 1921 the directors placed £10 at the disposal of Henry Hunt for special gratuities 'to any servant of the company for meritorious conduct in connection with the conveyance of troops, etc'. Next month, the authorities imposed a curfew in Derry, and on 22 April the *Derry Journal* gave a vivid description of a series of hold-ups on the Swilly :

TRAIN ATTACKED NEAR DERRY : FIRE OPENED ON RAIDERS

It is reported that the 8.20 a.m. mail train was held up yesterday at Inch Road Station, about seven miles from Derry, by armed and masked men. Two unknown men in civilian attire, who were passengers on the train, immediately opened fire on the raiders. The latter returned the fire, damaging part of the woodwork of the carriages. They then decamped, and the train proceeded. It is surmised that the civilians on the train were members of the Crown forces.

It was learned on Wednesday that the goods train which left Derry that morning shortly after 10 o'clock for Burtonport was boarded on arrival at Cashelnagore Station by three armed and masked men. This happened to be the last train over that section of the line, the service on which has been suspended by order of the military. One of the men going on the engine compelled the driver to proceed, and the other two men journeyed in the brake van. For some hours the train was missing and no information was available, the wires having been cut. Later it was learned that the train was halted at a point between Cashelnagore and Gweedore, where four additional armed men were waiting, and the waggons having been ransacked the raiders withdrew. Before leaving they stated that they were searching for Belfast goods, but nothing was interfered with. The train then proceeded to Burtonport.

An amazing sequel to the closing down of the railway took place on Wednesday night. It seems that the majority of the stations on the section were visited by armed men, and vast quantities of goods were seized and taken away, apart from some consignments which were burned in the vicinity. On Wednesday a special train timed to leave Burtonport at 5 p.m. to clear up the section, which had been closed down for traffic, was detained by armed men, and did not proceed until 8.20 a.m. yesterday.

Another raid on the mail train from Derry occurred on Wednesday at Ballymagan station, about two miles north of Buncrana. Six armed men, some masked, appeared on the station platform and imprisoned the railway officials. The mails were then taken away and the train ordered to proceed.

Although the division of Ireland had taken place, disorders continued, but 'The Troubles' as everyone was calling them, now took the form of civil war in the Free State, with a rival political party and its irregular army seeking to gain control of the country. Probably associated with this stage of the unrest was a fire in the Pennyburn workshops on 1 March 1922, which brought most repair work temporarily to a standstill.

During the summer a small group of the Irregulars occupied the disused Rectory at Burnfoot, sallying forth and stopping trains when in need of supplies. The regular Free State Army soon took counter-action, and for a time the Swilly trains made their way to and fro across the Tooban flats through the whine of snipers' bullets with the passengers and engine crews ensconced on the floor.

February 1923 was a month full of trouble. On 7 February a hurricane blew up from the west and ripped across the wilderness of granite boulders called the Rosses, lying east of Burtonport. The 8.30 a.m. mixed train was making its way from Burtonport and near mile post 68¾ it met the full force of the gale as it travelled along a low embankment. Two carriages and a bogie wagon were lifted off the line, tipped and fell sideways down the bank. Only the engine, driven by James Deeney, and the third brake van were left on the rails, separated by a gap where the other three vehicles had been. The frightened passengers gathered together in the brake van while Deeney took the engine on to Crolly for help. By the time he returned, the brake van had also been blown off the line. Just to add further to the chaos created by nature, someone maliciously set fire to one of the carriages before it was brought back to Derry.

The month continued with an unsuccessful attempt to blow up the bridge across the River Swilly, near Letterkenny. Three days later the carriage and wagon shops were maliciously set ablaze. Napier gloomily took stock:

> We now have six carriages and one bogie wagon to rebuild, in order to make good the loss of rolling stock. . . . In my opinion this work cannot be done without outside assistance under two years, as the

Londonderry and Lough Swilly Railway Company.

CONSECRATION

—OF THE—

BISHOP-ELECT OF RAPHOE

At Letterkenny, on Sunday, 22nd July, 1923

In connection with above Cheap Excursion Tickets will be issued and Special Trains run as under:—

8.20 a.m. Burtonport to Letterkenny

From	a.m.	Return Fare
BURTONPORT	8.20	2/9
DUNGLOE	8.25	3/- · 2/7
KINGASSLAGH	8.31	2/5
CROLLY	8.48	2/11

8.15 a.m. Gweedore to Letterkenny

From	a.m.	Return Fare
GWEEDORE	8.15	2/8
CASHELNAGORE	8.33	2/7
FALCARRAGH	8.46	2/5
DUNFANAGHY	9.7	2/3

8.45 a.m. Creeslough to Letterkenny

From	a.m.	Return Fare
CREESLOUGH	8.45	1/9
KILMACRENAN	9.10	1/6
CHURCHHILL	9.20	1/-
FOXHALL	9.30	-/9
NEWMILLS	9.35	-/6

9.0 a.m. Londonderry to Letterkenny

From	a.m.	Return Fare
LONDONDERRY	9.0	2/-
BRIDGE END	9.12	1/9
BURNFOOT	9.16	1/6
CARROWEN	9.27	1/6
NEWTON C.	9.38	1/-
SALLYBROOK	9.53	-/9
MANOR C.	9.59	-/9
PLUCK	10.8	-/6

RETURN TRAINS

For Crolly, Kingasslagh, Dungloe and Burtonport, leaves OLDTOWN at — 6.30
For Dunfanaghy, Falcarragh, Cashelnagore and Gweedore, leaves L'KENNY at — 7.0
For Foxhall, Churchhill, Kilmacrenan and Creeslough, leaves L'KENNY at — 7.30
For Pluck, Manor C., Sallybrook, etc. and Londonderry, leaves L'KENNY at — 6.30

Tickets may be purchased at Burtonport Line Stations on SATURDAY, 21st JULY, and will be available for travelling on that day as well as on SUNDAY, 22nd JULY. Passengers may also return from Letterkenny on Sunday, 22nd July or Monday, 23rd July, 1923. Tickets at the above Return Fares issued at Londonderry and Intermediate Stations will be available only on Sunday, 22nd July, 1923.

☞ TIME SHEWN ABOVE IS SUMMER TIME.

QUICK SERVICE—— CHEAP FARES.

H. HUNT, GENERAL MANAGER.

---

bótar iarainn Doire agus Loc Suiliġ.

COISREACAN

EASBUIC ÚIR RÁTBÓTA AIS LEITIR CEANAINN

DIA DOMNAIŻ, 22AD LÁ IÚIL, 1923.

béID TICéTIS SAORA AGUS TRAENTAIS SPEISIALTA AR AN LÁ SEO TUAS.

8.20 a.m. Gaot Dobáir go dtí Leitir Ceanainn

	maidin ticeto	dúbalta
Áit an Corráin	8.20	2/9
An Clocán Liat	8.26	3/- · 2/7
Ceann Caslaig	8.31	2/5
Croicslíge	8.48	2/11

8.15 a.m. Gaot Dobáir go dtí Leitir Ceanainn

	maidin ticeto	dúbalta
Gaot Dobáir	8.15	2/8
Caiseal na sor	8.33	2/7
An Fál Carraċ	8.45	2/5
Dún Fionnacaiġ	9.7	2/3

8.45 a.m. Craosloc go dtí Leitir Ceanainn

	maidin ticeto	dúbalta
Craosloc	8.45	2/3
Cill Mac Henáin	9.10	1/6
Mín an Labáin	9.20	1/-
Focshall	9.30	-/9
An Muileann Úr	9.35	-/6

9.0 a.m. Doire go dtí Leitir Ceanainn

	maidin ticeto	dúbalta
Doire	9.0	2/-
Druim Mumeadáin	9.12	1/9
Baile ron dá Adaim	9.16	1/6
Cárr eoġainn	9.27	1/6
Baile núá an Daoil	9.38	1/-
Sallidráċ	9.53	-/9
An Macáire Mór	9.59	-/9
Pluc	10.6	-/6

TRAENTAS-DÚBALTA

Go dtí Croicslíge, Ceann Caslaig, An Clocán Liat agus Áit an Corráin — 6.30
Go dtí Dún Fionnacaiġ, An Fál Carraċ, Caiseal na sor ┐ Gaot Dobáir — 7.0
Go dtí An Muileann Úr, Focshall, Mín an Labáin, Cill mac Henám agus Craosloc — 7.30
Go dtí Pluc, An Macáire Mór, Baile ron dá Adaim agus Doire — 6.30

Is féidir na ticétí a ceannać ag Stad Ráilrúin ar Líne Áit an Corráin Dia Sat., 21ad Iúl, agus is féidir úráId a baint arta ar an lá sin agus Dia Domnaiż 22ad Iúl le n-a coir. Is féidir teact ar ais Dia Luain 23ad Iúl. na ticétaí ruaza ó Doire agus ó na Stadiúns toimheatonaca, ní féidir úráID a baint arta act amáin aġ Dia Domnaiż 22ad Iúl, 1923.

☞ Is é am safráID an t-am seo tuas.

SEIRDÍS SASCA—— TICéTIS SAORA.

H. HUNT, BAINISTEOIR.

condition of some of the existing carriages will not permit of our concentrating on this work alone, and I would recommend that it be seriously considered whether some of these carriages should be built by an outside firm, as I have no hesitation in saying that when the carriage shop is rebuilt and in working order, a very great effort will be required to maintain the existing stock in a safe and satisfactory condition, to meet the requirements of the traffic.

The directors would not authorise this outside help, probably because they were more than a little uncertain whether they would ever get compensation for the damage. Besides, Trew Colquhoun, who had succeeded Brice Mullin as chairman in 1923, had at the March meeting described the previous 12 months as 'the worst year in history'. The Swilly had made a loss of £22,637. So Napier had to make his 'very great effort' unassisted, and to his credit had the damaged workshops back to normal by the end of May. His efforts were frustrated by a strike of some craftsmen for higher pay beginning on 2 May 1923. Engine repairs being completely suspended, cuts were again made in the service. But by the end of June the men were back at work, their wages unchanged.

As if the Company had not enough to bother them, Border Customs Posts came into operation in April 1923. The joiners, out of work as a result of the fire, were temporarily lent to the permanent-way department to assist in building a shed for the IFS Customs at Tooban, where goods traffic was examined. Passengers were dealt with at Bridge End. In Northern Ireland the Imperial Customs operated at first from Pennyburn, and later moved to Gallagh Road, and then in February 1924 when this halt was closed, back to Pennyburn.

The last serious malicious derailment took place on 24 September 1925, when the 11.25 a.m. ex-Derry ran into boulders at m.p. 68¼ between Crolly and Kincasslagh Road. The engine (No. 5) and carriage (No. 4B) were derailed but only superficially damaged. The crew, with the help of the two passengers, re-railed the train and it arrived at Burtonport only 90 minutes late.

CHAPTER X

Railway Supremacy Ends

FAHAN PIER AND THE LOUGH STEAMERS

From its opening in 1868, Fahan Pier had been the railway's property. The steamers on the Lough were operated by several different companies until 1877, when they were taken over by Messrs McCrea & McFarland, who the following year formed the Lough Swilly Steamboat Company with services between Fahan and Ramelton, Rathmullan and Portsalon, on the western shore of Lough Swilly. In April 1879 the Swilly Board discussed goods and passenger rates and agreed that the only vessels trading within the Lough allowed to use the pier, over which a railway siding had been laid down, should be those of McCrea & McFarland. The pier might, however, be used by other vessels trading outside the Lough. It was to be put into good order, and maintained by the railway, who agreed to put a two-ton crane on it.

A great gale practically destroyed the pier on 7 January 1920. For a time Buncrana pier was used instead, but as it had no goods accommodation, goods were booked to Fahan and stored there. Naturally Sir John McFarland pressed that the pier should be rebuilt as soon as possible, but the two Derry firms asked to quote refused to tender since they regarded it as past salvaging. So McCrea & McFarland were asked to lease and repair it. But nothing happened during 'The Troubles', and in March 1922 the Company decided to build a new pier using their own civil-engineering staff. Work began in the first week of May 1922, and finished by the end of the year. The old pier was straight; the new one had a wooden seaward part set almost parallel to the shore.

In November 1920 Sir John McFarland (then aged 81 with failing health: his partner Basil McCrea had died 14 years earlier) asked the railway Board if they would consider buying the Steamboat Co., the ferry rights and houses at Fahan and Rathmullan. The Company's vessels were the Preston-built paddle boat *Lake of Shadows*, then 16 years old, and two motor boats. The paddle boat was brought around to the Derry Graving Dock for inspection, and once a satisfactory report had been given, the Steamboat Company was purchased for £7,000—in February 1923. For the first time the railway operated their own marine services. Considering the unsettled state of the country and the poor financial position, it was a brave gesture.

The marine services was certainly not a money-making concern. The Swilly made a profit on the Lough services only on nine occasions in 29 years. They were, however, determined to keep a transport line open to the western shore of the Lough, even if it were unprofitable in itself.

GOVERNMENT ASSISTANCE

Under the combination of Trew Colquhoun as chairman, and Henry Hunt as manager, the Swilly faced the Irish peace that came in mid-1923. The civil war had ceased and the strike of craftsmen in the Pennyburn workshops was over. From the end of June 1922, the Order in Council which in 1917 had appointed Hunt as manager of the Burtonport Extension had been cancelled, and with that Tatlow's supervision had ceased as well. Wartime Government control came to an end in August 1921, when the IREC ended its direction.

But like many other lines, the Swilly found themselves with a post-war legacy of inflated operating costs due largely to the high rates of pay which had been brought into existence during the Government control. During that time no direct payment had been received for the transport of naval and military personnel and stores; railway companies were guaranteed the same net earnings as in 1913. Obtaining this 'post-war credit' turned out to be a prolonged affair, eventually settled by the Irish Railways (Settlement of Claims) Act of 1921. Irish railways as a whole received the round sum of £3,000,000. The Swilly's share came to £68,000, mainly appropriated towards losses in working in 1921, 1922 and 1923.

Despite these payments, withdrawals had to be made from the Company's reserve funds. Liquid reserves were exhausted by 1925. Indeed, in February 1924 the drain on the Swilly's purse had become so heavy that Colquhoun and Hastings of the Board, together with Sir John McFarland and his son Basil, lent the Company £2,500 to meet current expenses. The Board ordered that all expenditure was to be avoided except to keep the line 'in reasonable working condition'. Meantime the holder of ordinary shares saw the 7 per cent dividend, upon which he had depended since 1898, reduce to 5 per cent in 1921 and 3½ per cent in 1922. In 1923 there was no dividend, nor any distribution on preference stock.

The writing was on the wall. Yet because the roads were shockingly bad and social conditions in the old 'Congested Districts' offered less attraction to operators, road competition was not felt so early as in the more populous east of Ireland. In October 1920 Henry Hunt had unwittingly sealed the fate of the Carndonagh Extension by closing it in protest against the 'Munitions Strike'; such local men as owned lorries, or could raise the money to buy them, grasped the opportunity and started a free-for-all haulage service. Apart from anything else, it had novelty. The public responded to the local men's enterprise, and the Swilly never regained its traffic. But road transport had a long way to go before closure of the Extensions could be contemplated, though it was abundantly clear that neither of them would become profitable again.

Thus in 1924 the Irish Free State Government were approached for a grant. Since the Extensions had been State-subsidised in their building, the principle might well extend to their working—a dogma which their proposers had certainly never envisaged 25 years earlier.

After much consideration, the Free State Government conceded a proportion of the previous year's losses, perhaps hoping that the factors which had led to the losses would somehow or other alter. This did not occur. Road competition continued to grow, while the new tariffs had a restrictive effect on cross-border trade in both directions. To keep the patient alive, further transfusions were necessary, and the Free State grant was continued year by year. From 1925 an equal contribution was also made by the Government of Northern Ireland, who had to admit that if the line was not kept open the trade of the city of Derry would suffer. Both in 1924 and in 1925 the two grants totalled £14,000. Each year the Swilly's affairs were scrutinised closely by officials of both Governments before a further grant was authorised.

The high winds that sweep across the bleak west of Donegal from time to time had already derailed Swilly trains on four occasions when, in early 1925, the worst of these mishaps occurred. Between Kilmacrenan and Creeslough the line crossed a broad, marshy valley on the Owencarrow viaduct. A westerly gale was gusting down the valley when the 5.15 p.m. Derry to Burtonport train crept across the viaduct. The carriages were lifted bodily, and carried over the parapet wall. A light six-wheeler fell upside down on the rocks forming a short embankment, its roof came away, and four of the passengers within it were killed. Being an 'Act of God', the Company could not be held responsible, but a number of ex-gratia payments were made, amounting with attendant expenses to over £2,000.

CO-EXISTENCE AND REORGANISATION

By 1927, the wisdom of having two separate narrow-gauge systems in County Donegal was being questioned, and the Swilly directors approached the CDRJC to see if they would take them over. The Donegal sent their No. 3 railcar on a tour of inspection of the Swilly's line, driven by Ross Parks. In March 1928 the Donegal Committee formally decided not to carry the negotiations any further. Possible amalgamation was again studied in 1930, under Government auspices. Both the Swilly and the Northern Government would have welcomed it but again no action was taken, and the interesting prospect of a unified narrow-gauge system of nearly 225 miles vanished for the last time.

It is interesting to contrast the attitudes of the L & LS and the CDRJC. The latter concern was jointly owned by two great railway companies and was under the management of Henry Forbes, a fighter, whose policy for his railway's survival had become evident during the rough handling of his men and his line during 'The Troubles'. He went around armed and had shown that he was prepared to draw his revolver in defence of his timetable. Hunt, on the other hand, was a politician, characteristically wearing a theatrical cloak and backing up his position with an unparalleled command of strong language. Forbes only closed parts of his line under the strongest provocation, and though he was a 'Six County man', the Donegal staff respected him for it. Hunt, the Englishman, closed his line for far less reason and generally proved himself the less adaptable of the two managers. In Hunt's defence let it be said that many of his actions may have been guided by his directors, and theirs by what they could afford.

By 1928, working on a shoe-string, Forbes was experimenting with a petrol railcar for passengers and mails; by the end of that year he was running three railcars, learning as he went along. By 1931 the Donegal Railway had graduated to diesel railcars, albeit with the Great Northern's mechanical backing, and their pioneering and progress must today be acknowledged as brilliant.

Not until 1931 did the Swilly venture a look into the railcar field; they sent Napier across to Stranorlar to 'obtain information on rail

motor cars' with a view to using them on the Burtonport line. In
September 1931 Messrs Armstrong Whitworth quoted the Swilly for
two diesel-electric rail motors at £2,343 each. No action was taken.

During the late 1920s the day-to-day work of the Swilly went on,
in spite of a minimum of maintenance and scant ability to make
good the parsimony of the pre-war years and the ravages of war
and time. In 1929, eight years after similar action by the Donegal,
second-class travel was discontinued, and the seating was demoted
to third class. At the same time, first-class fares were reduced in an
effort to attract business and to stem the continuing fall in traffic.

By the end of the year 1930 the Company had been reduced to a
state of insolvency; they were heavily indebted to the bank, partly
secured by personal guarantee of the directors and by an almost
worthless debenture stock certificate for £8,000 as collateral secur-
ity. Many other creditors were involved, including heavy hire-
purchase commitments for vehicles.

After eight years' subsidisation by both Governments, it had
become painfully evident that a new approach to the problem of
the Company's survival was essential.

Henry Hunt's managership abruptly ended in May 1931. His
conduct had come under the scrutiny of the Board, and he was
given the opportunity of resigning and receiving a gratuity; so the
Swilly saw their dramatic Englishman no more. James Whyte, who
had been with the Company since 1910—as accountant since 1921
—was appointed Hunt's successor. A native of Fahan, he had grown
up within sight and sound of the line and he energetically attacked
the task of reorganisation.

The same year—1931—a scheme was formulated by the Company which had the approval of both Governments. Its essence was
that the Company undertook to acquire competing road services
within the area, then worked by private enterprise, with a view to
the eventual closure of the railway. For their part, the two Governments agreed to a further limited period of subsidies on a modified
scale. The change quickly produced satisfactory results. The loss on
railway working of £11,044 in 1930 was reduced to £3,823 in 1931.
The road transport services began to pay after 1931, yielding profits
averaging between £3,000 and £4,000 in the next five years. The
profits, however, were immediately swallowed up in paying off
accrued debts, and in providing new vehicles.

An ill-advised ten-week rail strike from the end of January 1933
dealt a body blow to the whole Irish railway organisation, and
finally sealed the fate of the Swilly railway. The strike affected all

train crews and outdoor staff. Clerical staff and stationmasters were not involved, but in self-defence, the impoverished Company gave them two weeks' notice. Then, in October 1933, having lost much of their goods traffic to private lorries, the Swilly reacted and gave notice of withdrawal from the Irish Railway Wages Board. As a result the guaranteed week of 48 hours was abolished, and many of the striking railwaymen were re-employed only part-time. The initial steps necessary to close down the Carndonagh Extension were also taken. As a prelude the Company acquired 54 road operators carrying goods as well as passengers between Derry and north and north-west Donegal. By the end of 1935 they were all co-ordinated into an entity designed ultimately to supersede the railway. The general legislation permitting these developments embodied an important basic principle: specific authority to close any section of the railway was conditional upon the Company providing adequate alternative road services for both passengers and goods.

Not everything was plain sailing. In the spring of 1931 an attempt was made to extend the west Donegal bus service to Dungloe and Burtonport. After eight weeks, during which the atrocious roads and the buses thoroughly hammered each other, the Company was forced to terminate the service some 20 miles short of Burtonport, at the village of Gortahork. The Donegal County Council claimed that the buses had damaged the roads and demanded £710 compensation. The claim was amicably settled for £120, but the Company had to undertake not to run regular bus services in the area in future without the County Council's permission; for a time they were forced to restore a limited train service over the entire Burtonport Extension. One train ran from Londonderry to Burtonport while a bus from Londonderry provided a connection for an additional Letterkenny—Burtonport working.

The next year, 1932, occasional derailments occurred on the Burtonport line, and to maintain it as economically as possible, second-hand sleepers and rails were bought from various sources: in April 1932, 150 tons of rails were obtained for £624, and in November 1933, 200 tons came from the Silent Valley Reservoir in County Down at £3 7s 6d per ton. Then in August 1935, 4,000 sleepers were purchased from T. W. Ward Ltd of Sheffield, who were dismantling the Keady—Castleblayney section of the Great Northern Railway. More sleepers came in 1936 off the Galway—Clifden branch of the Great Southern Railways. The best of the sleepers from the Carndonagh Extension went over to the Burtonport line, some worn ones being used as paling posts.

The Carndonagh Extension was closed completely on 30 November 1935, after which passenger trains on the old Swilly 'main line' from Tooban to Buncrana were confined to summer Thursdays and Saturdays, the expanding bus services now coping with most traffic, although a full train service was to be restored in the war. Four months earlier, the Swilly had sold a piece of land near Carndonagh station for a Government-built factory to produce industrial alcohol from potatoes—to the cynical, a legalised poteen still. This did not generate any worthwhile traffic, and provided employment only for a few. After the Extension's closure, a successful claim for compensaton was made by the owner of a stone quarry near Drumfries who had relied on a railway siding to get his stone away.

THE SWILLY IN WORLD WAR II

The arrangement allowing the British to maintain certain port installations in the Free State terminated in October 1938. Among the 'Treaty Ports' relinquished were Dunree and Leenan on Lough Swilly, no longer available as a British naval base. Another source of traffic disappeared. An outcome of the withdrawal, incidentally, was the offer by the British military of a 20-seater bus for £160. Although this had been used largely in the Free State, upon transfer of ownership it became liable to customs duty of £147; despite this drawback it was purchased and used up to 1950.

During the first world war the railway had enjoyed its virtual monopoly of transport, and although the line and its rolling stock were not in the best of condition, ordinary shareholders had received their 7 per cent dividend. By 1939 the Swilly's rail services were an admitted liability, to be shed just as soon as the county's roads could carry the rest of the traffic. The standard of maintenance of the permanent way, the engines and the rolling stock had been decided by economy. In spite of the changing picture the statistics of available engines, carriages and wagons had altered remarkably little since 1914. After 25 years the engine stock was only down by one, the number of carriages had lessened from 44 to 32, while passenger seats were reduced from 2,165 to 1,566. The number of wagons was the same before both wars. The whole picture indicated remarkable under-utilisation.

World War II affected the Company in a peculiar way, for the bulk of its railway mileage, 80¾ miles of first track, was in the neutral Free State. Over in Great Britain, Government control of the railways was imposed immediately war began, but Northern Ireland did not formally follow suit, and in the Free State the situation simply did not arise. As we have just seen, British troops evacuated the Swilly forts the previous year, to be succeeded by small detachments of Free State troops. The line had no expectation of appreciable military traffic.

The first year of the war, or 'the emergency' as it was called in the Free State, had little effect, and steps to end the remaining rail services began on 3 June 1940 with the closure of the entire Burtonport Extension (and the withdrawal of the last passenger working between Londonderry and Letterkenny) on the authority of a Government Statutory Order. An occasional goods train worked through to Burtonport until the end of July, but in August the firm of George Cohen & Company started the removal of the line—from the Burtonport end.

An increasing storm of public protest arose when the folk of the Rosses saw their rail link begin to vanish, and in October 1940 at a meeting of the Donegal County Council the railway's right to lift the Extension was challenged, it being asserted that it was still public property—unlike the Swilly's own line. A month later protest meetings were held at various places, and words were translated into action at Crolly, when a crowd of over 100 men closed the level-crossing gates, preventing the demolition train from moving. The Civic Guards and a Member of Parliament intervened, the Member guaranteeing that lifting of the track would cease until the whole question was examined and a ruling obtained from the Department of Industry and Commerce in Dublin. On 26 November it was announced that the Government had approved the lifting.

But by now the restrictions in petrol and oil imports resulted in rationing on both sides of the Border, and members of the Lough Swilly Board had misgivings about the demolition of the rest of the Extension. Authority was sought from the Irish Government to re-open from Letterkenny to Gweedore. It was then discovered that the Government had no power to revoke the Statutory Order made for closure; re-opening could only be by the Company's own volition and on their own financial responsibility. Since a decrepit railway was better than nothing at all, the Board reprieved the remains of the Extension and the Letterkenny—Gweedore section came to life again for goods traffic on 3 February 1941, a public-spirited act much appreciated by the Donegal folk. With the run-down of bus services, passengers were carred by the daily Londonderry—Gweedore goods train from March 1943.

In 1942 a full service of passenger trains was restored to the

G

Buncrana line and became increasingly well filled. The statistics for 1930-50 illustrate the changing pattern:

Year	Ordinary Tickets Issued		Passenger Receipts
	1st	3rd	(£)
1930	8,393	228,160	10,665
1935	869	112,244	5,126
1938	161	80,332	3,473
1939	49	61,063	2,920
1940	7	51,738	1,643
1941	nil	118,423	4,678
1942	9,415	337,246	18,617
1943	30,367	415,359	23,403
1944	34,148	408,529	24,059
1945	36,419	412,421	24,510
1946	24,855	333,932	19,821
1947	20,875	326,089	19,577
1948	14,789	241,989	14,540
1949	228	28,225	1,443
1950	nil	8,809	499

The extraordinary feature was the increase in first-class travel between 1942 and 1948, reflecting the enhanced spending power of the Derry wage-earners and their determination to make use of the best that the Swilly could offer—in a class of carriage that ran empty in 1941. In 1945, the peak year for first-class travel, the tickets amounted to 8.1 per cent of the total sold, although in the same year the first-class seats formed only 5.9 per cent of the available total of 1,340.

In April 1941 Derry city was attacked by German aircraft. Many houses were damaged, and a bomb narrowly missed the Swilly's headquarters at Pennyburn; little damage was done to buildings, but 100 carriage windows were broken. An immediate result of the bombing was the evacuation of large numbers of people to the surrounding area, especially neutral Donegal. This led to heavy commuter traffic into Derry. In 1940, with passenger trains on the Buncrana line only at weekends, no season tickets were issued. Between 1942 and 1945 the number was always over 250, including up to 25 firsts. People remaining in the city were keener than ever to get to the seaside on public holidays. On Bank Holidays in 1942, for instance, the two 4—8—4 tank engines were hard at work hauling packed trains of day trippers to Fahan and Buncrana.

Goods receipts did not increase so spectacularly. The aggregate tonnage of what was officially termed 'merchandise' (mainly coal, coke, cattle food, fertilisers and lime, potatoes, hardware and machinery) was about 25,000 annually between 1936 and 1940, which rose to 30,000 to 35,000 tons from 1941 to 1946. Coal produced revenue from £250 to £750 in the pre-war period. Wartime restrictions on exports of British coal resulted in its disappearance; in 1945 only 70 tons of coal passed over the Swilly, all originating outside the system and earning the Company a mere £15. Cattle traffic increased somewhat during food rationing in Northern Ireland, but did not attain much importance. It had fallen seriously in the last ten years before the war; back in the 1920s the average number of head moved had been about 24,000—coming in frantic bursts at the times of the local cattle fairs.

In 1941 the Company's net income was £17,352, and in the next seven years it rose to between £19,000 and £20,000. In 1942 a 1 per cent dividend was declared on ordinary shares (the first for 20 years) which was repeated in 1943. In 1944 it rose to 2 per cent, and in 1945 began a nine-year spell at 5 per cent. But little of this was due to the mild wartime revival of railway working.

I. J. Trew Colquhoun, chairman since 1924, died in 1944. His place was taken by Col. Sir Basil McFarland, Bt, who had just returned from five years' war service. He had joined the Board in 1921, four years after his father's resignation.

TURF IN THE TENDER

No account of the Swilly in the war would be complete without mention of the effect of the coal shortage on the railway's own motive power.

Between 1935 and 1940, the Company spent about £3,750 yearly on locomotive coal. By 1944 this was £13,000, to some extent the result of increased mileage but mainly due to the higher cost of coal. But the cost was one of the least worries. At times of acute shortage, another fuel had to be found. Oil was out of the question, and of course peat was the only solution. Peat makes an excellent slow fire in a flat domestic hearth, but is not at all the thing for an engine firebox as the draught lifts the pieces of turf off the bars. But it burns, and for six years the Swilly were glad of it. In 1943 and 1944 the situation became so desperate that even wood was burnt, though the resulting torrent of sparks from the chimney more than once set fire to wagon covers. For one week there was no coal at all.

Some of the turf was cut by the permanent-way staff from the Company's land adjoining the track. Larger quantities were bought in from the extensive bogs of west Donegal. Records of the issues and costs illustrate how extreme the shortage of coal became during this period of 6½ years, particularly when the comparatively low heating power and the bulkiness of turf are remembered:

1942:	Buncrana	832 t.	3 c.	2 q.		Cost:	£1,343	13s	3d
	Gweedore	979	6	0			£1,296	5s	0d
	Letterkenny	123	0	0			£184	10s	0d
1943:	Buncrana	124	0	0			£234	1s	0d
	Letterkenny	306	10	0			£494	3s	3d
	Creeslough	18	14	0			£31	5s	1d
	and	71	9	0	of wood		£113	8s	9d
	Gweedore	331	17	0			£529	4s	8d
1944:	Buncrana	257	12	0			£437	8s	0d
	Letterkenny	374	0	0			£622	14s	2d
	Creeslough	55	4	0			£90	12s	1d
	and	24	12	0	of wood		£41	9s	4d
	Gweedore	728	8	0			£1,275	14s	3d
1945:	Buncrana	164	15	0			£341	16s	1d
	Letterkenny	262	10	0			£519	7s	4d
	Creeslough	11	12	0			£19	1s	0d
	Gweedore	550	2	0			£970	4s	10d
1946:	Buncrana		nil						
	Letterkenny	39	0	0			£43	2s	9d
	Gweedore	76	0	0			£119	16s	1d
1947:	Buncrana	109	12	1			£315	9s	8d
	Letterkenny	14	0	0			£20	0s	0d
	Falcarragh	24	10	0			£86	6s	0d
1948:	Falcarragh	38	0	0			£185	18s	3d

The dependence of the Company on British coal had earlier been demonstrated during the General Strike, when Hunt had been forced to give the entire staff 14 days' notice, although complete closure was narrowly averted by a small allocation of coal from the stores of several Londonderry firms.

THE BURTONPORT LINE CLOSES

Goods trains continued to work to Gweedore throughout the 'emergency'. Although a little re-sleepering was done, no rails were replaced after 1943, and minor derailments became increasingly common, especially in dips where the track was on a curve and the unbraked wagons got a 'rug' as the couplings tightened on the ascent. A circular was sent to the engine crews in 1945, but there was little they could do.

By mid-1946, after six years of operation under stress of wartime conditions, and eight years after it had been condemned, the condition of the Letterkenny—Gweedore section was so bad that the Company requested the Government in Dublin to send their Railway Inspecting Officer, Mr T. C. Courtney (later chairman of Coras Iompair Eirann), to inspect the line. A quick examination with Mr Whyte served to convince him that it was dangerously dilapidated. He hastened back to Dublin, and reported that it should be put out of business immediately. So the regular goods service from Letterkenny to Gweedore was withdrawn on 6 January 1947. It took some time to establish the alternative lorry services and during this period certain special trains had to be run, but the section was finally closed in June 1947, not, of course, without protests.

The prolonged demise of the Burtonport Extension was full of interest to students of railways and it is a pity that it missed much publicity it would undoubtedly have received ten years later. We can now only regret that no-one ever came forward to offer the Company the scrap value for a typical Burtonport engine—all maintained in remarkably good mechanical condition. At the time, unfortunately, there was no Transport Museum in Belfast; use on the neighbouring Donegal line was never seriously contemplated. Eventually the engines were cut up for scrap.

This is part of one of the few written records of the Burtonport road:[1]

We set off with the regulator set at second port and cut-off about 75% (third notch) which was increased as the gradient stiffened, after the preliminary run down into Dunfanaghy Road. This formidable bank is three-and-a-half miles long at an average of 1 in 50, and engines of No. 2's class are only allowed to take 100 tons over it. Here the elements can make life distinctly unpleasant for the engine crew, but this time they were kind to us and the ascent was made in grand style, steam never falling below 130 lb. under the beetling shadow of Muckish. . . . The telephone wires have been removed from Falcarragh, and the line is worked now by either 'bush telegraph' or, more probably, on the understanding that one engine only is allowed beyond here!

Glorious glimpses of Tory Island on our right and the Derryveagh Mountains on the fireman's side were ours as we proceeded towards Errigal, but Driver Clifford had more to do than admire the view! His chief trouble was stray sheep, and he scared most of them off with the draincocks and the whistle. Usually this only had the effect of herding them into the 'three foot' just a bare length ahead of the engine and quite spoilt what might have been a grand descent into

[1] *Railway Magazine*, 1949, p. 353

Gweedore now only half a mile away. . . . At Gweedore, the now familiar procedure of pulling up well short of the station, uncoupling the locomotive and using her for advance shunting duties, was adopted. When these are completed, the screw brake in the van is eased and the train runs down into the platform; as the guard says, 'It's useful having all your stations in the dip!' . . .

As a sad but interesting sequel to the journey to Gweedore in 1946, I was privileged to travel with the demolition train when it crossed Owencarrow Viaduct for the last time. On Tuesday, July 19, 1949, I joined Driver Harrigan (who had been our fireman in 1946) on the footplate of No. 12 . . . and by 11 a.m. we had drawn out of Letterkenny with a train consisting of a wagon, four flats (actually the frames of passenger vehicles) and a brake composite coach. Grass growing on the track made the running far from easy, and only frequent use of the sanders enabled us to breast the 1 in 50 gradients between Letterkenny and Kilmacrenan. After some shunting at Kilmacrenan, the engine propelled the train.

Near the foot of the ascent to Barnes Gap, we stopped again to take water from a small river, through a petrol-driven pump carried in the van. This procedure was necessary because the track already had been removed at Creeslough, the nearest station with a water tank. No. 12 climbed to Barnes Gap in fine style, and then we made a cautious run over the serpentine descent to the viaduct. A short distance beyond the viaduct, the track ended abruptly and only a bare path of ballast extended across the bog to Creeslough.

Men were soon at work loading the train, and by 2.30 p.m. the last train ever to cross Owencarrow Viaduct began its return journey, with a full load of rails and sleepers.

LAST SIX YEARS OF RAILWAY WORKING

With the Extensions trimmed away and the bulk of passenger and freight traffic moving by road, the Swilly's railway was now reduced to what it had been in 1883, a total of 30¾ miles of first track. On the Buncrana line, owing to the difficulty of getting sufficient buses, the public were at first offered both a passenger and a goods service. The Letterkenny line carried only goods, but since there were no goods brake vans, the trains included a passenger brake and that had a few compartments to seat people wanting to travel.

During 1947 on weekdays, four passenger and two mixed trains were run from Derry to Buncrana, with an additional mixed train on a Saturday. In the up direction there were five passenger and one mixed trains during the week, plus three mixed on Saturdays. On Sundays two passenger trains ran in each direction. Out to Letterkenny were the two goods trains. The busiest scene on the system took place at Tooban Junction for a few minutes around 11.50 a.m.

on Saturdays, when the 11.30 a.m. mixed ex-Buncrana, the 10.45 a.m. goods for Letterkenny and the 10.40 a.m. goods ex-Letterkenny all crossed.

The August Bank Holiday traffic in 1947 was as busy as ever, with five daily trains in each direction. On Tuesday 5 August, for instance, the evening up trains from Buncrana were heavily loaded: No. 10 hauled six coaches on the 5.5 p.m., No. 5, 13 coaches on the 7.45 p.m., and No. 8 ten coaches on the 8.45 p.m. At such times the end of the railway seemed far away. A passenger special also ran in mid-November for the Letterkenny Hiring Fair.

The same passenger workings were repeated next year. On 3 August 1948 a post-war record was made on one of the evening trains returning to Derry from Buncrana, for on arrival at the terminus there emerged from its crowded coaches 1,146 passengers.

In September the passenger services were tapered off since sufficient buses had become available. First the weekday services were withdrawn, leaving a limited train service on Saturdays and Sundays to the end of that month. Thereafter all regular passenger services ended, though specials were still worked at holiday weekends.

The 1950 August Bank Holiday workings were disappointing. On Saturday 5 August only 100 passengers were carried, though the next day brought around 1,000. On Bank Holiday Monday about 600 persons used the trains, and 200 on the Tuesday. The following year was the last time that these excursions were run. The travelling habits of the Derry folk were altering even on holidays; private cars were coming back in increasing numbers and the Swilly's buses were well filled.

The final goods services on the Buncrana line consisted of an 11 a.m. run from Buncrana to Derry which returned to Buncrana at 1.15 p.m. After an hour at Buncrana, the engine worked traffic as far as Tooban Junction at 3.30, where it exchanged vehicles with the 2.15 p.m. ex-Letterkenny, and then returned to Buncrana at 4.15. The engine then ran light to Fahan, where it was shedded. On the line between Derry and Letterkenny, two goods trains ran in each direction, six days of the week.

In January 1953, the great gale that sank the *Princess Victoria* on her crossing from Stranraer to Larne caused heavy damage to the stone pitching that protected the line just north of Fahan. The line was undermined and had to be closed for three days; the foundation of the permanent way there was merely rubble laid across the sand and it had given occasional trouble from the time the line was built.

THE SWILLY ENDED QUIETLY . . . JUST LIKE THAT

That the increased road services carried the dying railway on their back is best illustrated by this table of net earnings and the Company's dividend:

Year	Road (£)	Rail (£)	Dividend (per cent)	
1930	−48	− 10,821	nil	Reorganisation 1931
1935	3,729	− 3,762	nil	Carndonagh Ext. closed
1940	1,764	2,340	nil	Part B'port Ext. closed
1941	16,047	2,352	nil	
1942	18,360	787	1	
1943	16,877	1,928	1	
1944	11,408	422	2	
1945	18,989	3,115	5	
1946	15,612	− 2,826	5	
1947	20,433	− 3,721	5	Closure of B'port Ext. completed
1948	14,995	− 4,246	5	
1949	22,696	− 12,000	5	
1950	15,958	− 4,602	5	
1951	17,210	− 6,266	5	
1952	11,940	− 6,244	5	
1953	12,634	− 5,721	5	Rest of rly. closed
1954	5,236	− 1,131	6	
1955	6,539	—	7	
1956	14,079	—	7	

The end was inevitable. As soon as road goods services were adequate, early in 1953, formal application was made to the two Governments for the necessary closure Orders. The last trains were expected to run both to Buncrana and Letterkenny on 1 July 1953. There was, however, some delay in obtaining the Order from the southern Government, and trains continued until Saturday 8 August. The final run into Buncrana was the 4.15 p.m. out of Tooban, hauled by No. 10 which was driven by Dick Quinn with Hedley Connell firing. The 2.30 p.m. for Letterkenny ex-Derry was driven by John Hannigan, with his brother Leo firing. Last train of all was the 2.15 p.m. from Letterkenny, heavily loaded with 14 wagons of cattle and into Derry 50 minutes late. It was headed by the Carndonagh engine, No. 15, with Bob Turner driving her and Paddy Clifford firing. The reporter of the *Derry Journal* travelled on the footplate on the last lap, and wrote:

As the train halted for a minute on the outward side of the Strand
Road level-crossing gates, the guard, Mr. Daniel McFeeley, or anyone
else, did not call out 'Next stop Derry'. Everyone knew that the next
stop would be the last—the last ever.

The train was watched by hardly a score of persons as it rumbled
over the level-crossing and along the final few hundred yards of grass-
grown track into the almost roofless terminus. The platform at which
it drew up was deserted.

On its left stood the adjoining track, and there one saw parked a
few rail tank cars and coupled to them a few passenger coaches,
empty, old and of indefinite colour—silent reminders of the days when
the old station was alive with the laughter of thousands of excursionists, and when those faded coaches were newer.

With the driver's rag in his hand Robert Turner made his last
adjustment at the engine, and the train pulled up. 'That's the end,' said
our reporter. 'That's the end,' he smiled back. The Swilly Railway
service ended quietly, just like that.

CHAPTER XI

The Course of the Line

LONDONDERRY TO BUNCRANA

For much of the railway's life, the terminus was close to the Graving Dock belonging to the Harbour Commissioners. In its later state this station had two platforms, with the usual offices housed in a thoroughly plain, rough stone building. Badly lit, and in a cramped situation between the Strand Road and the harbour tramway, it was never the subject of complimentary remarks. From 1869 until 1888, apart from a short spell in 1885, trains by-passed it, apart from Sundays, and worked along the Harbour Commissioners' line to the Middle Quay. No permanent station buildings were erected there, the only accommodation being an uncovered wooden platform, although a wooden goods shed may have done duty for a time.

From Graving Dock to Pennyburn level crossing, the line ran between Strand Road and the quays, separated from both by high stone walls. The road crossing was oblique. A signal cabin once stood at the north-east side but was not replaced when demolished to make room for a power station building. Pennyburn had no crossing place. The line curved towards a north-westerly course with the single platform on one side and the railway workshops and sidings on the other. A short way out of the yard, the last houses of Derry were left behind. After a mile the line passed

THE STATION PLANS

The following symbols are used in plans of stations in this chapter.

AH	agent's house	S	station buildings
C	customs office	SB	signal box
CP	cattle pens	TS	tarpaulin tarring shed
GF	ground frame	TT	turntable
GS	goods store	W	water column
LB	loading bank	WS	waiting shed
LS	locomotive shed	WT	water tank
LX	level crossing		

GRAVING DOCK LONDONDERRY
c. 1945

Harbour Tramway

S

GS

LX

Pennyburn

CP STRAND ROAD

WORKSHOPS

ROAD

1 2 3/4 5

TT WT

COAL DUMP

Tooban Junc.

LS

WORKSHOPS
1. CARRIAGE & WAGON
2. SMITHY
3. MACHINE SHOP
4. LOCO. SHOP
5. STORE

TS

OFFICES

PENNYBURN, LONDONDERRY
c. 1945

STRAND ROAD

LX

JOINERS SHOP   FITTING & ERECTING SHOP   STORES STABLES   SWITCH RM.

ROAD

LS

Tooban Junc.

5'3" gauge

WT TT

CRANE

CP

STRAND ROAD

PENNYBURN, LONDONDERRY

Proposed new terminus (Act of 1918)
from an L. & L.S. drawing dated
13 February 1918.

COAL STAGE

GS

S

LX

beneath the main road, nor far from Collon House, where the 1891 collision occurred.

From Collon through Bridge End to Burnfoot the track was almost straight and level. Two miles out, Gallagh Road station was placed just beyond a level crossing where a minor road led to the hamlets of Upper and Lower Gallagh. The 6 in. Ordnance map spells the station 'Gallagh Road', but the hamlets and the townland 'Galliagh'. The 1864 timetable used the latter spelling, but later editions used 'Gallagh'. The local pronunciation was 'Gal-yah'.

The short-lived Harrity's Road station or halt was at the next level crossing, a short way beyond which the railway crossed the boundary into County Donegal. Approaching Bridge End, the line began a two-mile traverse of rather marshy country, relic of the old tidal sloblands that were reclaimed by the Trady, Inch and Farland Embankments. The district between Burnfoot and Bridge End is still known colloquially as 'The Light Water'.

Bridge End station stood at an important level crossing and drew in traffic from a wide area on both sides of the valley. It had a large goods store, in a part of which the Free State Customs had their office. Bridge End was not a proper crossing place, though the short goods loop was so used from time to time. The platform and the two-storey agent's house were on the down, or north side. A water tank was provided.

At Burnfoot (where before the embankments were built the Lough ran up to within a few yards of the village street at a high

Gradient profile Londonderry—Carndonagh

tide) the station had a single platform on the side next the village, with a single-storey agent's house and a small store. Past Burnfoot the railway kept between the cut courses of two small rivers, along the north side of the old slobland until reaching Tooban Junction, surrounded by the flat marshlands of Inch Level. The station was on the site of one for the Farland and the Buncrana lines in the railway's early days. When rebuilt in 1883 for the opening of the Letterkenny Railway, it had an island platform 240 ft long. From June 1883 to March 1885, the junction (then referred to as Letterkenny Junction) had the 5 ft 3 in. gauge line of the Swilly along its north face and the 3 ft gauge line of the Letterkenny along its south face. Thereafter narrow-gauge lines flanked it, the left hand or south road being used by down trains, the right or north road being taken by up trains. At the end of the platform was a scissors crossover, separating the Buncrana and the Letterkenny roads. The down starter signal had two arms on one post, an economical arrangement, but unusual since the Buncrana arm pointed to the right of the line.

This station was referred to in public and in working timetables simply as 'Junction' until after 1920, when the prefix 'Tooban' was officially used. It had no vehicular access and was primarily an exchange point between the two lines. It never had a nameboard, and no tickets were printed. The lofty signal cabin at the Derry end of the platform was a place of recourse for many a train crew waiting for the road; in latter years the cabin was under the charge of a character named John Doherty, or more familiarly 'The Rattler'. Tooban could be pleasant on a warm summer day, when dragonflies played over the marshlands, but it was an eerie enough place, and a lonely one, in the dark of a winter's night.

Less than a mile out of Tooban, Inch Road station was placed where two roads converged on the embankment that linked Quigley's Point on the mainland with Inch Island. The station had a single platform on the west side of the line, and a short siding. For the next two miles the railway ran close to the tidal channel on the landward side of Inch Island. A short stone platform was made along this stretch about 1927, to serve a cluster of houses, and was named Lamberton's Halt. Immediately ahead were the woods around Glengollan House, and after a short causeway the line ran beside a low rocky bluff and into Fahan station.

Fahan in Irish is spelt Fothain, which means the sheltered place, and the village is charmingly situated along the southern, tree-covered slope of Gollan Hill. Near the north-western end, a gravel

GALLAGH ROAD

AH

SIDING DISCONNECTED
PRIOR TO 1946

Derry   LX   Tooban

BRIDGE END   FROM LLSR PLAN (UNDATED)

C   GS

Derry

SB   WT   WS   AH   LX   Tooban

BURNFOOT (TOOBAN) JUNCTION   FROM PLAN BY G.P. CULVERWELL 1 MAY 1883

Road

Burnfoot River

Buncrana   Derry
Letterkenny

SITE OF EARLIER 5'3" PLATFORM

Skeog River

TOOBAN JUNCTION

Road

Burnfoot River

Buncrana   Derry
SB

L'kenny   LB
GS+C

Skeog River

FROM LLSR PLAN, 6 FEB. 1923

spit reaches into the tideway towards Inch Island, and at the end of it the old Farland Point pier was re-erected in 1868. Despite the importance of boat connections to the railway, the station had but a single-platform, reached by stone stairs from the road overbridge, on the west side of the line. On the level triangle of land behind it stood the usual offices, stationmaster's house, some dwelling houses, a corrugated iron goods shed, and a locomotive shed—once a coal store for a local merchant. A small wooden signal cabin covered the ground frame at the north end of the platform, and beyond it a line trailed in to the left towards the pier. A trailing spur off this siding ran to the locomotive shed, and another spur along the south side of the spit was used as a wagon siding.

Soon after leaving Fahan station the line curved to the right through a short, deep rock cutting, and emerged on an exposed part of the coast, much open to the north-west gales. The sea's erosion of the sandy subsoil necessitated constant permanent-way mainten-ance. This section was almost completely obscured by road widen-ing in 1963. After about a mile, the line had the protection of the Lisfannon Links, where a golf course was built. Mainly for golfers, Beach Halt was a short wood-faced platform at the south end of the links. Half a mile to the north Golf Halt, renamed Lisfannon Links, was opened in 1892 beside the club house, and had a crude sema-phore signal which was raised to stop approaching trains.

Now within sight of Buncrana, the line curved northward to the station of two platforms joined by an overbridge, the down plat-form being long enough to hold two trains; turntable, water column and goods store were provided. In the days of the herring fishing, the station was seasonally extremely busy, with fish curing depots and sheds on the railway's land, between the line and the sea. No drawings exist of the station in its original state, but in spite of damage by fire in 1905, it was a fine building of squared local stone, with quoins and dressings of yellow brick and it presented an impressive two-storey frontage to the county road at the southern edge of the little town.

BUNCRANA TO CARNDONAGH

From Buncrana, the Carndonagh Extension curved to the right and crossed the main road obliquely, to face seven miles of almost unbroken climbing. At first the swift-flowing Mill River lay to the left, but within a few hundred yards the line, rising at 1 in 60, swung to the north and crossed the river by a high five-arch

masonry bridge, close to Swan's Corn Mills. It then passed along the east side of the little town and shortly reached open country. Two miles out, Ballymagan station was sited on the right, just before a road overbridge. The station buildings were typical of those on this section, which were the best on the entire system: neat masonry walls of quartzite, well built in squared rubble, with quoins and dressings in yellow brick. The roofs were slated, with a ridge of ornamental red tiles.

After Ballymagan the line soon entered open bogland and crossed the meandering Crana River by a single-span lattice girder bridge. Kinnego Halt was placed in 1930 at a gate house on a branch off the main Buncrana road half a mile to the left.

Now on gentler gradients, but with mountains rising on both sides, the line rose to Drumfries where a few houses clustered round a road junction. The station buildings and the main road were on the left, or west side. Ahead was the picturesque and reed-girded Mintiaghs Lough: the railway kept to the eastern shore and the road to the west. A short way north of the lough, a minor road led into the hills, and here, at Cochrane's siding, was a loading bank for stone. The scenery grew quite spectacular as the summit level of 332 ft above sea level was reached. The jagged crags of Barnan Beg and Barnan More, overhanging in places, reared skyward and made a dramatic backcloth to the quiet shores of the lough.

Railway and road now ran close together on the four-mile descent, guided by the valley of the Clonmany River. The three-arch Meendoran Bridge took the track over a sheltered bend in the stream. Not far past it, on a steeply descending section, was Meendoran Halt, at No 5 Gates, 3¾ miles from Drumfries.

Clonmany station was the block post and passing point on the Extension, and was located on a hill slope half a mile south-east of the village. It served a considerable hinterland, and was the station for the two military camps in this district during World War I. The station buildings, on the down platform, were similar to those at Ballymagan and Drumfries, but were slightly larger.

The next two stations, at Ballyliffin and Rashenny, were located beside road level crossings. Both places were favoured by tourists visiting the magnificent strand three miles to the north. Between the two stations, the line dropped towards sea level at 1 in 50. It has been stated that Ballyliffin station was Ireland's 'furthest north', but Rashenny, almost two miles nearer Carndonagh, was exactly a quarter of a mile further north. Much of the last four miles lay close to the shores of Trawbreaga Bay. A halt, officially named

H

GS LB CP S WT
WALL ROAD
Buncrana C'donagh
SB WS

GLONMANY
FROM CONTRACTOR'S PLAN

ROAD
GS LB
AH S
Buncrana Carndonagh
PLATFORM EXTENDED C. 1927

BALLYLIFFIN
FROM L.L.S.R. PLAN, 3 NOV. 1927

CARNDONAGH
FROM CONTRACTOR'S PLAN

CP ROAD
CS LB
GS
TT LS
W
Buncrana
SB WT
AH S

NEWTONCUNNINGHAM from G.P. Culverwell's plan, 4-1-1883

WS
W
L'kenny WELL W Derry
WT AH +S
ROAD
CP
GS

Carndoagh, and locally Collin Hill, was built at an overbridge to serve a few nearby houses. Beyond, the line turned towards the south-east, and rose a little on the final 1½-mile run into the terminus, on the north side of the little town of Carndonagh.

THE LETTERKENNY RAILWAY SECTION

On leaving Tooban Junction the line curved to the left and joined the great Trady Embankment. On the left, the featureless salty flats of Inch Level stretched for a mile or more to the foot of the hills crowned by the Grianan of Aileach. Once on the top of the embankment the railway kept a straight and practically level south-easterly course for almost a mile to Trady station, where a small islet existed prior to the reclamation work. The track then veered almost east, and keeping beside the water, continued towards the meeting of the Trady and the Farland Embankments. Close to the flood gates, the old line to Farland sloped down gently to its terminus a quarter of a mile away. Nearly a century after its abandonment, clear traces can still be seen of the low embankment along the sandy shore. The stone wall of the old turntable pit is still in place, overgrown with grass and saplings. At the Point itself, the massive stone facing is in almost perfect condition on the east side and a few timber stumps remain as witnesses of the pier that saw the first Swilly trains arrive, and was then dismantled and taken to Fahan.

Returning to the end of the Trady Embankment, the junction between the original L & LS and the later Letterkenny Railway was located at the west side of the townland of Inch Level, near the boundary against the townland of Carrowen. Perhaps because the place is in the electoral division of Burt it has been called Burt Junction, though this was not the official name and the spot was not marked. Once on to the old Letterkenny Railway, the track curved south-east, away from the Lough, and rose at 1 in 49 through a deep earth cutting before running along a low embankment into Carrowen. This station had a simple, single platform, a cottage for the agent, and a short siding.

Not far past Carrowen, the line approached an inlet of Lough Swilly named Blanket Nook, which was partly reclaimed by the Grange Embankment, and crossed the shallow bay along a causeway. A series of minor undulations followed and then 3½ miles from Carrowen the trains entered Newtoncunningham station, a block post and the most important intermediate station on the Letterkenny Railway. It had two platforms, a good two-storey

NEWTONCUNNINGHAM
around 1950

SALLYBROOK

from LLSR plan, 26·5·37

MANORCUNNINGHAM

from G.P. Culverwell's plan, 4·1·1883

LETTERKENNY
around 1950

station building and agent's house on the down platform, a goods yard, cattle pens and water columns.

Leaving Newton, as the station was named, the line faced a climb of three miles, with some sections as steep as 1 in 60. By the summit, near milepost 16, it had risen almost 200 ft; Sallybrook station was then entered. It had a considerable goods traffic in connection with the Lagan Creamery.

Dropping steeply, with the rich farmlands of the Lagan on each side, the line took a westerly course and reached Manorcunningham, merely a roadside platform, nearly two miles south of the village it served. Next came Pluck station, not far from a small village of that name, beyond which the railway circled the base of a rounded drumlin. Then within sight of the salt flats and mud banks where the River Swilly joined the Lough, railway and road kept together for the four miles into Letterkenny, losing height down some 1 in 50 sections on the way. A mile from the town the Strabane & Letterkenny Railway came in on the left and crossed the Swilly to reach its terminus. It was on this last section of the Letterkenny Railway that the first of the 'blow-offs' took place, on 28 January 1884.

The Letterkenny Railway station was at the fork of two roads, at the eastern extremity of the town's mile-long street. The s & l obtained powers to wedge their station immediately to the north. To some latter-day visitors, the sight of the two stations side by side was ludicrous. But in 1910, at the height of their powers under John McFarland's guidance, the Swilly were in no mood to co-operate with their rival.

THE BURTONPORT EXTENSION

Before it could head north-west, the Extension had to circumnavigate Letterkenny, heading south-west, between the town and the meandering loops of the River Swilly, over flat land liable to winter floods. The first station, Oldtown, was a small affair serving the west end of Letterkenny and its older neighbour, Oldtown, on the hill to the south.

The line now followed the sheltered and well-wooded valley of the River Swilly for three miles, first crossing to the south bank and then back to the north before entering Newmills station. This second river crossing was the start of the first hard climbing. Setting a north-westerly course, the line worked higher on the south-facing slope of the Swilly valley until, a mile past Newmills, it turned abruptly north into a tributary valley and 5¼ miles from Letterkenny came to Foxhall station, named after a nearby estate. There was no village, the station serving only the scattered small farms in the neighbourhood.

All of the way from Newmills to the No 2 Gates, half a mile past Foxhall, the gradient had been an almost unbroken 1 in 50 and 200 ft had been gained. To No 3 Gates came easy running, to be followed by a steep descent beside the Glashagh Burn into Churchill station, placed in the broad valley of the Glashagh, where the line crossed a moor road to Churchill village 1½ miles away. Once the Glashagh River was crossed, there was stiff climbing, with sections at 1 in 50 to a summit approximately 340 ft above the sea; and then into Kilmacrenan.

Not until ten years after the opening did Kilmacrenan become a block post in the middle of the 21-mile section from Letterkenny to Creeslough. The original station was to the east of the line, with a goods siding making a trailing junction towards Letterkenny. The platform became the up one, a loop and a down platform being added to the west, with a neat stone waiting shelter and a store. The goods siding had the usual cattle pens, store and loading bank, and also had a loop serving a secondary loading bank for bog-iron ore traffic. The village was 2½ miles to the east. Not far from the station is the famous Doon Rock and Holy Well, the scene of pilgrimage for hundreds of people seeking its reported miraculous healing powers. Near the Well is the Rock of Doon, where the chiefs of Tyrconnell, the O'Donnells, were crowned. Special trains were run for these pilgrimages, not only over the Swilly, but also from parts of the County Donegal system.

Leaving Kilmacrenan on a falling gradient, the Loughsalt Mountains could be seen ahead. A mile north of the station, in increasingly wild and rocky country, the line curved north-west, making for a narrow pass between Stragraddy Mountain and Crocknacrady. The main road and railway converged to a level crossing in Barnes Upper townland, and it was here, at No 8 Gates, that Barnes Halt stood from 1927 until 1940. The climb continued at 1 in 55 to a summit near 40¼ m.p., after which a long descent at 1 in 50 began. For two miles road and railway ran close together, into the bleak, rock-strewn Barnes Gap, where railway crossed road by a viaduct 60 ft high with three 60 ft spans. There, at the northern opening of the Gap, with a 10 m.p.h. speed restriction, the trains swung west, crossing the road by a viaduct and emerging on the desolate, boulder-covered, south-east slope of the valley of the Owencarrow River. The view suddenly broadened, with the white quartzite cone

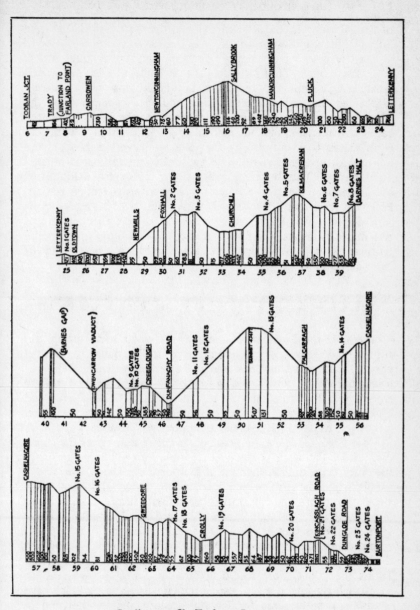

Gradient profile Tooban—Burtonport

of Errigal rising to 2,466 ft ten miles to the west, and the massive
bulk of Muckish closer at hand.

The Owencarrow River flows north-east and links Lough Veagh
and Glen Lough, falling 44 ft in a distance of five miles, and
meandering on the flat, marshy valley floor. This valley squarely
obstructed the path of the builders, and they spanned it by the
380 yd Owencarrow Viaduct. The approach to the viaduct from the
south was rendered difficult not only by the persisting 1 in 50 fall
from Barnes Gap, but also by the 13-chain curve that brought the
line round through a right angle and on to the approach embankment. Rising 40 ft above the valley floor, and entered and quitted
by rock embankments, the viaduct was a curiously composite affair.
Followed from south to north, it was made up of 15 girder spans
(three being 139 ft 3 in. in length), a short stone embankment, and
two masonry arches. The falling gradient persisted to the end of the
tenth span, the eleventh span was level, and then a rising gradient
of 1 in 50 followed.

Once over the Owencarrow the line traversed a rock cutting, and
surmounted a small gable before dropping to Creeslough, the second
passing place and block post out of Letterkenny. The station was
beside the village, which was on the trunk coast road, and it drew
extensive traffic from the east to the shores of Sheep Haven and
Mulroy Bay. It was the nearest station for Rosapenna Hotel
(destroyed by fire in 1963) and its famous golf course.

From Creeslough, falling gradients brought trains over the three-
span girder Faymore Viaduct, 50 ft high, into Dunfanaghy Road,
six miles from the small town of Dunfanaghy. The station was a
simple single platform, with a goods siding. The tidal inlet of Sheep
Haven was nearby; at the station the railway turned sharply away
from the trunk road and immediately began a four-mile climb at
1 in 50; the summit level of 474 ft came shortly after m.p. 50,
where an embankment was succeeded by a short rock cutting and
the line curved around a hill and alongside the lonely Lough Agher.
Trains then once more lost height in an almost straight run to
Falcarragh station, at a spot called the Fiddler's Bridge, which gave
tourists access to some fine coastal scenery and beaches and to
Falcarragh village, four miles away. The railway was now well
among the wild scenery of the 'Donegal Highlands'. The gradients

became more broken on the climb, which took the line to Cashel-nagore three miles past Falcarragh.

Cashelnagore station, 420 ft above sea level and the highest on the system, was reputed to be the only two-storey building in the whole neighbourhood. To the north, the land falls away to the Gleen River valley, dotted with numberless whitewashed cabins, their thatched roofs well tied down against the winter gales. The valley, cut up by dry stone dykes into tiny fields, stretches away to the northern coast at Bedlam and Gortahork. Ahead as the railway left Cashelnagore, the lovely cone of Errigal reared skyward. A mile to the south-east of Cashelnagore station, Aghla More Mountain rose sheer to 1,804 ft from Altan Lough. All around was the wildest of the Donegal landscape, grim and bleak in winter, but beautiful and colourful in summer.

Six miles beyond Cashelnagore, reached for the most part over falling gradients, was Gweedore station, where there was a good hotel but no village. The station, serving the scattered coastal popu-lation of the Bloody Foreland, Derrybeg and Dunlewy, was a block post, with two 70 yd platforms and a goods siding. From 1940 until 1947 it was the terminus of the Extension, and as it never had a turntable the tender engine (No. 12) had to work back tender first. A rear weather board was added to give the crews some protection.

Leaving Gweedore, trains turned south across to the Gweedore River valley, in sight of the sheltered cottages of Dore and the island-studded coast at Inishfree Bay. Curving around from south to south-west and on falling gradients the train entered Crolly, a single platform, with a small carpet factory as the local industry.

For the last ten miles to Burtonport, the railway was in the dis-trict known as the Rosses, consisting of some 60,000 granite-strewn acres, intersected by streams and with more than a hundred lakes filling hollows in the almost treeless landscape. The population is scattered, with only two centres of any size: Annagary in the north and Dungloe on the south coast. With characteristic perversity, the railway ignored both these places, heading to Burtonport as directly as the land surface allowed. The traverse was unsheltered, gradients varied, and short rock cuttings alternated with low em-bankments laid across patches of waterlogged peat bog. Just over half way across the Rosses a halt, Kincasslagh Road, was opened in 1913 at No. 21 Gates in Meenbanid townland. Here the railway passed between two small loughs, a mile inland from the intricately indented coastline at Keadew Strand.

Dungloe Road was at the nearest approach to the village, but was

CHURCHILL
from undated LLS plan

GS CP
AH WS
L'kenny LX Burtonport

CREESLOUGH
from undated L.LS. plan

Letterkenny
WS AH WT
B'port
W GF WS
WOOD
CP GS
LB
ROAD

FALCARRAGH
from an L.L.S. plan dated
30.8.1917

ROAD
LB
S GS
CP
Burtonport LX
L'kenny
RIVER

SIDING AND LOOP RESITED ON OTHER
SIDE OF GOODS SHED C.1925

BURTONPORT

from undated L.L.S plan
(Carriage Shed later removed)

SHORE
TT WT LS
Quay
CS GS LB
GF
Letterkenny
WS AH
CLIFF

four miles north-west of it, at the north end of Lough Meala. Now on low ground, the train passed the last pair of crossing gates, and half a mile from the terminus the railway emerged from the rocky wilderness to the coast, running past weed-strewn creeks, and by short rock faces of warm red granite. A level course brought the rails past the distant and home signals, the turntable and the engine shed, and alongside the single platform of Burtonport station.

The terminus was something of an anticlimax. There was little but the harbour at Burtonport. The station accommodation was of the simplest, a two-storey, stone-built agent's house, backing on a granite bluff, with a little waiting room alongside. The goods store and the loading bank faced out to sea, and the line serving them continued close to the edge of the water, past fish packing and curing sheds to the head of the pier. The entire area occupied by the terminus and sidings was laid on an uneven rocky shore, and required great quantities of rock material to fill and level it. Today, even after a quarter-century of neglect, the massive stone pitching is still perfectly sound.

Postscript: Along the Carndonagh Extension, on the lonely stretch of line near the Kinnego Gates, stories are told of the appearance of a ghost train. The train, made up of an engine, two carriages and a brake van, is supposed to have been seen on at least three occasions and on one such the crossing keeper hurriedly opened the gates for what he took to be an unannounced special. Nearer to Buncrana, the same phenomenon was seen by one Dan McLoughlin at No. 1 Gates, where it passed completely through them.

CHAPTER XII

Working the System

TRAIN SERVICES

In February 1864 trains ran on weekdays only, leaving Derry at 7.30 a.m. and 4.0 p.m., and Farland at 8.20 a.m. and 5.0 p.m. (soon changed to 7 p.m.). The journey took 35 minutes. There was an additional 'special' at times varying according to the tides.

The steamer played an important part in the transport network. In May it began with the departure from Thorn at 6.45 a.m. A Ballylin call was made at 8.10 a.m. and it then went to Farland to meet the 8.0 train ex-Derry. It took on passengers, goods and livestock and recrossed to Ballylin. During the middle of the day it did a run from Farland to Ramelton and back, in connection with the variably-timed train (Ramelton quay up the River Leannan could not be reached at low tide), and then got back to Ballylin in time for the 5.0 p.m. sailing to Farland. At Farland passengers from the steamer had to wait about 90 minutes for the 7.0 p.m. to Londonderry, and must have been glad to avail themselves of the comfort of the refreshment room in that remote spot. Meanwhile the steamer took passengers off the 5.0 from Londonderry to Ballylin and up the river to Thorn, where at 7.0 it tied up for the night. Except on the variably-timed service, Ramelton passengers joined and left the steamer at Ballylin, four miles away. There was no pier here, since reference is made to steamers 'calling off Ballylin'. Heavy goods would have gone by the variably-timed service to Ramelton's excellent pier. Thorn was advertised as 'Thorn for Letterkenny'.

Road connections were arranged with the steamer calls. 'Cresswell's Van' travelled between Ballylin and Ramelton, and 'Diver's Van' between Thorn and Letterkenny. The railway timetable also gave notes on both the cross-channel and the transatlantic services from Derry.

Until the Buncrana branch was opened, a 'car' ran on Wednesdays and Saturdays only between Heron's Hotel in Buncrana and Burnfoot station, meeting the morning train to Derry and the evening service back. Once the line was opened to Buncrana, four trains were provided in each direction. This line quickly became more important than that to Farland, which for a time was worked by horses. Soon the Farland branch workings ended, when a more reliable steamer service was provided at Fahan in 1868. During the next seven years the Buncrana service appears to have been four up and down trains in summer, cut back to three in winter. In 1875 the fourth service ran throughout the year. Sunday trains ran in summer from 1865.

When the Letterkenny Railway opened in June 1883 a single train left the terminus at 8.0 a.m., connected at Tooban with a Buncrana train, which was in Derry by 9.50 a.m. On the return, passengers left Derry at 4.15 p.m. and were at Letterkenny at 6.05 p.m. At first it was not possible to get from Derry to Letterkenny and back in a day, but from November 1883 three trains were provided each way over the Letterkenny line. For some years after the Derry—Buncrana line was narrowed, Letterkenny passengers usually had to change at Tooban. The 1888 timetables (overleaf) tell their own story.

When the Carndonagh Extension was opened in 1901, there were seven weekday trains to Buncrana, of which the 6.30 and 11.50 a.m. and 4.30 p.m. were extended to the new terminus, running non-stop from Derry either to Tooban or to Inch Road. A short Derry—Tooban stopping train was run at 11.20 a.m., ahead of the 11.50 a.m. Carndonagh mail. A Monday market train, 9.15 a.m. Carndonagh—Clonmany, returning at 10.0, was added. Two all-station trains ran to Carndonagh and back on Sundays.

On the Letterkenny line in 1901, the first down train was the 4 a.m. mail, stopping at Newtoñcunningham and Manorcunningham and reaching Letterkenny at 5.18 a.m. The next two arrivals were connections off Carndonagh trains; finally there was a 90-minute through train leaving Derry at 5.15 p.m. The Letterkenny line had no Sunday trains then.

The Burtonport line opened on 9 March 1903 with two trains on weekdays and one on Sundays each way, soon increased to three daily at the insistence of the Board of Works. Thereafter arrangements on the entire system were fairly stable for a few years, save for the troubles which resulted in the Tatlow inquiries.

In 1916 the Swilly decided that, Board of Works or not, two trains per day to Burtonport were sufficient; but the Treasury successfully applied for an injunction to prevent the reduction. In evidence the railway stated that on four successive days in April

STATIONS.	DOWN TRAINS.			
	WEEK DAYS.			
	Pass'rs only.	Goods and Pass'rs	Goods and Pass'rs	Pass'rs only.
LEAVE	A. M.	A. M.	P. M.	P. M.
Derry, Middle Quay............	6 10	11 0		4 20
Gallagh Road	6 28	11 16		4 36
Bridge End	6 33	11 21		4 41
Burnfoot...........	6 38	11 25		4 45
Junction........................	6 45	11 32		4 52
Carrowen	6 55	11 42		5 2
Newtowncunningham	7 5	11 55		5 15
Sallybrook....................... ..	7 20	12 10		5 30
Manorcunningham	7 25	12 17		5 35
Pluck.............................	7 30	12 25		5 40
Arrive at Letterkenny	7 45	12 40		5 55

STATIONS.	UP TRAINS.		
	WEEK DAYS.		
	Pass'rs only.	Goods and Pass'rs	Goods and Pass'rs
LEAVE	A. M.	P. M.	P. M.
Letterkenny	8 0	1 50	7 40
Pluck	8 12	2 3	7 53
Manorcunningham...............	8 20	2 10	8 0
Sallybrook	8 25	2 16	8 6
Newtowncunningham	8 40	2 30	8 20
Carrowen	8 50	2 43	8 33
Junction	9 5	3 0	8 50
Burnfoot......	9 15	3 5	8 55
Bridge End.......................	9 20	3 10	9 0
Gallagh Road	9 25	3 15	9 5
Arrive at Derry, Middle Quay	9 40	3 30	9 20

The public timetables from 1 May 1888 are reproduced above and on page 127. Note the old spelling 'Newtowncunningham'.

DOWN TRAINS.

LEAVE	WEEK DAYS						SUNDAYS	
	Mail.	Goods and Pass'rs	Goods and Passr's	Goods and Pass'rs	Mail. Pass'rs only.	Goods and Pass'rs		
	A. M.	A. M.	P. M.	P. M.	P. M.	P. M.	A. M.	P. M.
Derry, Middle Quay	6 10	11 0	1 10		4 20	6 30		
Do., Graving Dock							9 45	3 30
*Gallagh Road............	6 28	11 16	1 26		4 36	6 46	9 50	3 38
*Bridge End..............	6 33	11 21	1 31		4 41	6 51	9 55	3 45
*Burnfoot	6 38	11 25	1 37		4 45	6 57	10 0	3 50
Junction	6 45	11 32			4 52			
*Inch Road..............	6 50	11 37	1 43		4 57	7 3	10 5	3 55
Fahan.....................	6 55	11 45	1 50		5 5	7 10	10 10	4 0
Arr. at Buncrana........	7 5	11 55	2 0		5 15	7 20	10 20	4 10

UP TRAINS.

LEAVE	WEEK DAYS						SUNDAYS	
	Mail.	noon	Goods	Goods and Pass'rs	Mail. Pass'rs only.	Goods and Pass'rs		
	A. M.	noon	P. M.	P. M.	P. M.	P. M.	A. M.	P. M.
Buncrana.................	8 50	12 10	2 40	5 30	8 30		10 35	8 30
Fahan	9 0	12 20	2 50	5 40	8 40		10 45	8 40
*Inch Road	9 5	12 25	2 55	5 45	8 45		10 50	8 45
Junction	9 10		3 0		8 50			
*Burnfoot.................	9 15	12 30	3 5	5 50	8 55		10 55	8 50
*Bridge End..............	9 20	12 35	3 10	5 55	9 0		11 0	9 0
*Gallagh Road...........	9 25	12 40	3 15	6 0	9 5		11 5	9 5
Arr. at Derry, Graving Dock							11 10	9 10
Do., Middle Quay	9 40	12 55	3 30	6 15	9 20			

1915 the 6.0 p.m. from Burtonport carried 9, 6, 11 and 39 passengers, earning 6s 1d, 5s 6d, 15s 8d and £2 0s 3d respectively, a funeral swelling business the last day. On the same days the 2.15 p.m. train had carried 24, 24, 22 and 73 passengers respectively. The train with 24 passengers yielded 15s 1d in fares, 1s 11d from parcels, 2s 6d from manure, 5s 10d from cattle, and 1s 3d from newspapers. The running cost was put at £4 15s 4d, making a loss of £3 8s 9d.

After Tatlow had made his 1917 recommendations, revised arrangements involved four trains on weekdays to Burtonport, three being the usual mixed, and one a goods and livestock only from Letterkenny. The 5.30 a.m ex-Derry was in Burtonport in 264 minutes and was the fastest down train. The 11.40 a.m. crossed the up trains at Letterkenny, Creeslough and Gweedore, and took 310 minutes to reach Burtonport. On Sundays there was a single train each way. At this time, Buncrana received six trains from Derry (plus a seventh on Saturday nights), of which three ran through to Carndonagh, with an extra morning working on Carndonagh market and fair days.

Services were drastically reduced in 1918, and even by 1922 (the date of the working timetables reproduced on the following pages) were not fully restored. Next spring (1923) three long hauls to Burtonport were reinstated every day. But all-the-year Sunday services over the entire system were not repeated after the war. Summer Sunday services were, however, introduced on the Buncrana line especially for Derry excursionists. Two trains left the city, an 11.30 a.m. that went on to Carndonagh and a 3.0 p.m. just to Buncrana. In the up direction the 8.30 p.m. from Buncrana was followed by the 7.45 p.m. ex-Carndonagh. The Buncrana trains were frequently run in duplicate on fine Sundays. There was also a 'short' excursion, out of Carndonagh, to take people to the beach near Ballyliffin. Worked by the Carndonagh engine, it left at 2.30 p.m. and ran only to Clonmany, where it waited until its return at 6.50 p.m.

It was the Carndonagh Extension that first felt the chill wind of retrenchment. By the end of 1931 only one mixed train went to Carndonagh even on weekdays, though the market and fair-day specials and a Wednesdays and Saturdays mixed ran out from Derry at 4.30 p.m., returning at 7.30 p.m. Four years later all services ended, and the buses and lorries handled the traffic north of Buncrana. By late 1931, Burtonport again received only two weekday trains, only one being a through service from Derry.

Once the Burtonport Extension had been cut back to Gweedore, two goods ran there daily. First out was the 8.30 a.m. ex-Letterkenny which was into Gweedore at 11 a.m. It was followed by the 10.10 a.m. ex-Derry, which left Letterkenny at 1.30 p.m. and was into Gweedore at 4 p.m. Departures from Gweedore were timed at 8.30 a.m. and 1.30 p.m., the former continuing on to Derry. There was also a stopping goods in each direction between Derry and Letterkenny. In contrast to the attenuated wartime service on the remains of the Burtonport Extension, the Derry—Buncrana service was heavy, with six passenger or mixed trains up and down on Mondays to Fridays, nine on Saturdays, and two on Sundays.

From the 1947 closure of the Letterkenny—Gweedore section, the Derry—Letterkenny section continued to be provided with two

LONDONDERRY—1

(1) *The Graving Dock terminus from Strand Road, April 1953*
(2) *Graving Dock platforms, looking towards Pennyburn, August 1952*
(3) *Graving Dock terminus No. 2 on 10 a.m. Burtonport train, July 1939*

LONDONDERRY—2

(4) *Middle Quay platform, from a photograph thought to have been taken in about 1883. The engine is one of the two 0—6—0ST type supplied by R. Stephenson in 1883 and later sold to the Harbour Commissioners*

(5) *Pennyburn level crossing and the last train, August 1953*

LONDONDERRY—3

(6) *Locomotive shed at Pennyburn. One of the Hawthorn, Leslie engines in front, May 1938*

(7) *Pennyburn shed. Platelayer's trolley on left. Offices and platform on right, level crossing in background, August 1952*

(8) *No. 10 approaching Pennyburn platform, August 1951*

BRIDGE END

(9) *No. 2 on down goods, August 1952*
(10) *No. 10 on 9.30 a.m. Derry—Letterkenny goods, March 1953*
(11) *Platform end, looking towards Burnfoot. Customs and goods shed on left,*
August 1952

TOOBAN JUNCTION

(12) *View towards Burnfoot. Nos. 10 and 2 on Buncrana and Letterkenny train, March 1952*

(13) *Two-arm signal at west end. Nos. 10 and 2 on Buncrana and Letterkenny trains, August 1952*

INCH ROAD—FAHAN

(14) *Inch Road station from No. 10 on 1.15 p.m. Derry—Buncrana train,
March 1953*

(15) *Fahan sidings and P.S. 'Innishowen' from pier, about 1903*

(16) *Fahan pier and Inch Island showing P.S. 'Innishowen' and at pierhead
P.S. 'Lake of Shadows' (on left) and P.S. 'Kate' (on right), about 1903*

FAHAN—BUNCRANA

(17) *Rock cutting north of Fahan station, Lough Swilly beyond*
(18) *No. 10 in Buncrana station, looking north, August 1952*
(19) *Signal box and sidings at south end, Buncrana station, No. 10 shunting, August 1952*

BUNCRANA IN 1948

(20) *Looking south*

(21) *Road frontage*

(22) *No. 15 leaving with 13-coach excursion*

THE CARN LINE

(23) *Meendoran bridge and 'J. T. Macky' on inspection run, about* 1901
(24) *Carndonagh station, arrival of first train,* 1 *July* 1901
(25) 4—6—2T *working pulsometer outside Carndonagh station*

WEST FROM TOOBAN

(26) *No. 8 heading up goods, on Trady Embankment, April 1948*
(27) *View along Trady Embankment from west end, June 1937*
(28) *Carrowen station, looking east, April 1950*

NEWTONCUNNINGHAM

(29) *Driver Turner boarding No. 15, as No. 2 approaches with up goods,*
March 1953

(30) *Crossing in snow. No. 8 brings in the 9.30 a.m. ex-Derry, while the*
up goods waits for the road, December 1952

LETTERKENNY

(31) *Goods store, platforms and signal cabin from No. 12, March 1953*

(32) *5.50 p.m. Letterkenny to Burtonport ordinary train (two L & LS coaches in rear) with seven coaches of CDRJC containing special school parties returning from outing to Strabane*

LETTERKENNY—KILMACRENAN

(33) *No. 14 arriving at Letterkenny with 8.30 a.m. train ex-Burtonport,*
May 1938
(34) *Barclay tank on 2 p.m. ex-Burtonport, approaching Foxhall, May 1938*
(35) *Kilmacrenan station from south. Goods siding to right*

BARNES GAP—OWENCARROW

(36) *Barnes Gap viaduct, looking north*

(37) *4—8—0 engine on up mixed train, crossing Owencarrow viaduct, about 1910*

(38) *Black Hawthorn engine (No. 2 or 3) on engineer's inspection train, south end of Owencarrow viaduct, about 1903*

CREESLOUGH—GWEEDORE

(39) *No. 12 leaving Creeslough with up train, June 1937*
(40) *No. 12 shunting, Gweedore, June 1937*
(41) *Gweedore station, looking east, about 1903*

BURTONPORT

(42) *The station, No. 14 on 8.30 a.m. train, May 1938*
(43) *No. 12 taking up train past loco shed, June 1937*
(44) *Siding from station to pier, June 1937*

DERAILMENT BY WIND

(45) *Wreckage of down train, derailed on Owencarrow viaduct,*
30 January 1925

(46) *Roofless 6-wheeled carriage No. 12 on west side of Owencarrow viaduct*
after derailment, 30 January 1925

(47) *Derailment near Crolly, 7 February 1923*

(48) 0—6—2T *No. 1, 'J. T. Macky'*

(49) 0—6—0T *No. 4, 'Innishowen'*
about 1900. J. Deeney in cab

(50) 2—4—0T *No. 6A partly dis-*
mantled at Pennyburn about
1900

LOCOMOTIVES—II

(51) 4—6—2T *No. 15 at Letterkenny, 1953*
(52) 4—6—0T *No. 4 in original livery, 1902*
(53) 4—6—2T *No. 10 in black livery, 1952*

LOCOMOTIVES—III

(54) 4—8—4T *No. 5 at Pennyburn, 1951*

(55) 4—6—2T *No. 14 in original livery, 1910*

(56) 4—8—0 *No. 12 at Pennyburn, 1935*

COACHING STOCK

(57) *LLSR No. 5 6-wheeled compo,*
Pennyburn 1937

(58) *LBER No. 12 & LLSR No. 18,*
Pennyburn 1950

(59) *LBER No. 1 in original livery,*
1902

WAGON STOCK

(60) *LBER covered wagon with centre canvas No. 45, 1902*
(61) *LBER timber truck No. 61, 1902*
(62) *Bogie covered wagon/brake No. 7 ex-LBER carriage, 1952*

ROYAL TRAIN—JULY 1903

(63) *Train on arrival at Middle Quay, Londonderry, from Buncrana*

(64) *4—6—2T No. 7 decorated and named 'Edward VII' at Buncrana*

(65) *BNCR saloon carriage in Pennyburn yard*

LONDONDERRY

AND

LOUGH SWILLY

RAILWAY.

NEXT TO SAFETY ..

PUNCTUAL RUNNING

OF TRAINS IS MOST

IMPORTANT.

WORKING TIME TABLE

(For the information of Company's Servants only.)

From MONDAY, 2nd OCTOBER, 1922,

and until further notice.

All previous Time Tables are hereby cancelled.

No alterations of the arrangements shewn herein must be made without the authority of the General Manager. Every Servant of the Company engaged in the working of Trains must carry with him a copy of this Working Time Table, a copy of the Appendix hereto, and a copy of the Company's Book of Rules and Regulations, and will be held responsible for understanding and properly carrying out the instructions contained therein, so far as they concern him in the execution of his duty.

H. HUNT,

General Manager.

PENNYBURN,
28th September, 1922.

Printed at the Sentinel Office, Londonderry

K

LONDONDERRY AND LOUGH SWILLY RAILWAY CO.

> **Next to Safety Punctual Running of Trains is Most Important.**

TRAIN SERVICE

(From 2nd OCTOBER, 1922, and until further Notice)

Burtonport and Letterkenny to Londonderry.

UP TRAINS.

Distance from Burtonport.		STATIONS.	No. 24 Passenger. Week Days.		No. 25 Passenger. Week Days.		*No. 26 Goods. (Alternate days to No. 22 as per advice).		No. 27 Passenger. Week Days.	
Mls.	Chs.		arr.	dep.	arr.	dep.	arr.	dep.	arr.	dep.
			a.m.	a.m.	a.m.	a.m.	p.m.	p.m.	p.m.	p.m.
		BURTONPORT ..				8 30		1 0		3 20
1	43	Dungloe ..			8 35	8 36		1 7	3 25	3 26
2	76	Kincasslagh ..			8 40	8 41		1 12	3 30	3 31
8	37	Crolly ..			8 57	8 58		1 30	3 47	3 48
11	50	**GWEEDORE**			9 8		1 40		3 58	
						9 13		1 54		4 6
17	59	Cashelnagore ..			9 30	9 31		2 16	4 23	4 24
20	79	Falcarragh ..			9 39	9 40		2 25	4 32	4 33
27	70	Dunfanaghy ..			10 3	10 5		2 50	4 55	4 58
29	4	**CREESLOUGH** ..			10 10		2 59		5 3	
					Cross No. 20					
						10 20		3 5		5 8
37	24	**KILMACRENAN** ..			10 46		3 30		5 33	
									Cross No. 22	
						10 48		3 35		5 36
40	73	Churchill ..			10 57	10 58		3 47	5 45	5 46
44	35	Foxhall ..			11 8	11 9		3 59	5 56	5 57
45	67	New Mills ..			11 13	11 14		4 4	6 1	6 2
48	76	Oldtown ..			11 21	11 23		4 17	6 9	6 11
49	56	**LETTERKENNY** ..			11 26		4 20		6 14	
									Cross No. 23	
				7 20		11 36		4 40		6 28
53	71	Pluck ..	7 32	7 33	11 48	11 49	Pass		6 40	6 41
55	72	Manor ..	7 39	7 41	11 55	11 56	Pass		6 47	6 48
57	59	Sallybrook ..	7 47	7 48	12 2	12 3	Pass		6 54	6 55
61	43	**NEWTON** ..	8 1		12 16		5 20		7 8	
			Cross No. 20		Cross No. 21		Cross No. 23			
				8 20		12 23		5 30		7 12
65	14	Carrowen ..	8 32	8 33	12 32	12 33	Pass		7 21	7 22
68	16	**TOOBAN JUNCTION** ..	8 39				5 50		Pass	
					Cross No. 2		Cross No. 6			
				8 49		12 40		6 20		7 29
69	22	Burnfoot ..	8 52	8 53	12 43	12 44	Pass		7 32	7 33
70	58	Bridge End ..	8 56	9 3	12 47	12 50	Pass		7 36	7 39
72	38	Gallagh Road ..	9 8	9 9	12 55	12 56	Pass		7 44	7 45
		Pennyburn ..		9 14		1 1		6 40		7 50
74	36	**LONDONDERRY** ..	9 15		1 2		6 41		7 51	

★ **Advice will be sent if this Train is to run.**

Next to Safety Punctual Running of Trains is Most Important.

LONDONDERRY AND LOUGH SWILLY RAILWAY CO.

TRAIN SERVICE

(From 2nd OCTOBER, 1922, and until further Notice).

Londonderry to Letterkenny and Burtonport.

DOWN TRAINS.

Distance from Derry.		STATIONS.	No. 20 Passenger. Week Days.		No. 21 Passenger. Week Days.		★ No. 22 Goods. (Alternate days to No. 26 as per advice).		No. 23 Passenger. Week Days.	
Mls.	Chs.		arr.	dep.	arr.	dep.	arr.	dep.	arr.	dep.
			a.m.	a.m.	a.m.	a.m.	p.m.	p.m.	p.m.	p.m.
		LONDONDERRY		7 30		11 30		2 0		4 45
1	78	Gallagh Road	7 36	7 37	11 36	11 37	as required		4 51	4 52
3	58	Bridge End	7 42	7 43	11 42	11 43	as required		4 57	4 58
5	14	Burnfoot	7 46	7 47	11 46	11 47	as required		5 1	5 2
6	20	TOOBAN JUNCTION	Pass		Pass		Pass		Pass	
				7 50		11 50		2 20		5 5
9	22	Carrowen	7 58	7 59	12 0	12 1			5 13	5 14
12	73	NEWTON	8 8		12 10		2 40		5 23	
			Cross No. 21		Cross No. 25					
				8 12		12 20		2 50		5 27
16	57	Sallybrook	8 27	8 28	12 35	12 36	as required		5 42	5 43
18	44	Manor	8 33	8 34	12 41	12 42	as required		5 48	5 49
20	45	Pluck	8 40	8 42	12 48	12 50	as required		5 55	5 57
24	60	LETTERKENNY	8 53		1 1		8 30		6 8	
				9 3				4 10		Cross No. 27
										6 20
25	40	Oldtown	9 6	9 7				4 15	6 23	6 24
28	49	New Mills	9 15	9 16				4 27	6 32	6 33
30	1	Foxhall	9 24	9 25				4 42	6 41	6 42
33	43	Churchill	9 34	9 35				4 54	6 51	6 55
37	12	KILMACRENAN	9 47				5 20		7 7	
							Cross No. 27			
				9 50				5 40		7 12
45	32	CREESLOUGH	10 12				6 5		7 35	
			Cross No. 25							
				10 19				6 20		7 40
46	46	Dunfanaghy	10 22	10 23				6 25	7 43	7 45
53	37	Falcarragh	10 49	10 51				7 0	8 11	8 13
56	59	Cashelnagore	11 2	11 4				7 15	8 24	8 26
62	66	GWEEDORE	11 19					7 40	8 41	
				11 29						8 46
65	79	Crolly	11 37	11 39				7 51	8 54	8 55
71	40	Kincasslagh Road	11 55	11 57				8 10	9 11	9 12
72	73	Dungloe	12 0	12 4				8 16	9 15	9 16
74	36	BURTONPORT	12 8				8 20		9 20	

★ Advice will be sent if this Train is to run.

TRAIN SERVICE
(From 2nd OCTOBER, 1922, and until further notice).

NEXT TO SAFETY PUNCTUAL RUNNING OF TRAINS IS MOST IMPORTANT.

DOWN TRAINS. Londonderry to Buncrana and Carndonagh.

Mls. Distance from Derry.	Chs.	STATIONS.	No. 1 Passenger. Week Days.		No. 2 Passenger. Week Days.		No. 3 Passenger. Saturdays only.		No. 4 Passenger. Week Days.		No. 5 Passenger. Mondays excepted.		No. 6 Passenger. Week Days.		No. 7 Passenger. Mondays only.		No. 8 Passenger. Saturdays only.	
			arr	dep	arr	dep	arr	dep	arr	dep	arr	dep	arr	dep	arr	dep	arr	dep
			a.m.	a.m.	p.m.	p.m.	p.m.	p.m.	p.m.	p.m.	p.m.	p.m.	p.m.	p.m.	p.m.	p.m.	p.m.	p.m.
		LONDONDERRY		7 15		12 20		2 30		4 0				6 0				9 0
1	78	Gallagh Road ..	7 21	7 22	12 26	12 27	2 36	2 37	4 6	4 7			6 6	6 7			9 6	9 8
3	58	Bridge End ..	7 27	7 28	12 32	12 33	2 42	2 43	4 12	4 13			6 12	6 13			9 13	9 15
5	14	Burnfoot ..	7 31	7 32	12 36	12 37	2 46	2 47	4 16	4 17			6 16	6 17			9 18	9 19
6	20	JUNCTION ..	Pass				Pass		Pass				Pass					9 22
				7 35	Cross No. 25	12 40		2 50		4 20				6 20				
7	6	Inch Road ..	7 38	7 39	12 43	12 44	2 53	2 54	4 23	4 24			6 23	6 24			9 25	9 27
9	17	Fahan ..	7 44	7 46	12 49	12 51	2 59	3 1	4 29	4 31			6 29	6 31			9 32	9 35
		Lisfannon ..	Pass		A		A		A				A				Pass	
12	15	BUNCRANA ..	7 55		1 0		3 10		4 40				6 40				9 43	
			Cross No. 9	8 20	Cross No. 13	1 9						4 50				7 0		
14	41	Ballymagan ..	8 30	8 31	1 19	1 20					5 0	5 1			7 10	7 11		
17	70	Drumfries ..	8 42	8 43	1 31	1 32					5 12	5 13			7 22	7 23		
23	0	CLONMANY ..	8 55		1 45						5 25				7 35			
			Cross	No. 11								5 30				7 40		
				9 1		1 49												
24	32	Ballyliffin ..	9 6	9 7	1 54	1 55					5 35	5 36			7 45	7 46		
26	14	Rashenny ..	9 11	9 13	1 59	2 1					5 40	5 42			7 50	7 52		
30	39	CARNDONAGH	9 25		2 13						5 54				8 4			

UP TRAINS. Carndonagh and Buncrana to Londonderry.

Mls. Distance from Carn.	Chs.	STATIONS.	No. 9 Passeng'r Wednesdays only.		No. 10 Passeng'r Week Days.		No. 11 Passeng'r Wednesdays excepted.		No. 12 Passenger. Week Days.		No. 13 Passenger. Mondays excepted.		No. 14 Passeng'r Week Days.		No. 15 Empty Stock. Sat'rd'ys only.		No. 16 Passeng'r Week Days.		No. 17 Passeng'r Mondays only.		No. 18 Passeng'r Week Days.	
			arr	dep	arr	dep	arr	dep	arr	dep	arr	dep	arr	dep			arr	dep	arr	dep	arr	dep
			a.m.	a.m.	a.m.	a.m.	a.m.	a.m.	a.m.	a.m.	p.m.	p.m.	p.m.	p.m.			p.m.	p.m.	p.m.	p.m.	p.m.	p.m.
		CARNDONAGH		7 10				8 30				11 55						3 30		5 30		
4	25	Rashenny ..	7 21	7 22			8 41	8 42			12 6	12 7					3 41	3 42	5 41	5 42		
6	7	Ballyliffin ..	7 27	7 28			8 47	8 48			12 12	12 13					3 47	3 48	5 47	5 48		
7	39	CLONMANY ..	7 32				8 52				12 17						3 52		5 52			
							Cross No. 1															
				7 37				8 58				12 24						3 58		5 58		
12	49	Drumfries ..	7 54	7 55			9 15	9 16			12 41	12 42					4 15	4 16	6 15	6 16		
15	78	Ballymagan ..	8 4	8 7			9 25	9 28			12 51	12 54					4 25	4 28	6 25	6 28		
18	24	BUNCRANA ..	8 14				9 35				1 1						4 35		6 35			
						8 25				9 45				1 10	3 15		Cross No. 5	4 50	Cross No. 6	6 50		7 30
21	22	Lisfannon ..			pass				A		A						A		pass		A	
23	33	Fahan ..			8 33	8 34			9 53	9 54			1 19	1 20			4 59	5 0	6 58	6 59	7 39	7 40
		Inch Road ..			8 39	8 40			9 59	10 0			1 25	1 26			5 4	5 5	7 4	7 5	7 45	7 46
24	19	JUNCTION ..			pass	8 43			pass	10 5			pass	1 29			pass	5 9		7 8	pass	7 49
25	25	Burnfoot ..			pass				10 8	10 9			1 32	1 33			5 12	5 13	7 13	7 14	7 52	7 53
26	1	Bridge End ..			8 49	8 52			10 12	10 15			1 36	1 39			5 16	5 19	7 17	7 20	7 56	7 59
28	1	Gallagh Road ..			pass				10 20	10 21			1 44	1 45			5 24	5 25	7 25	7 26	8 4	8 5
		Pennyburn ..			pass	9 2				10 26				1 50	3 49			5 30		7 31		8 10
30	39	LONDONDERRY		9 3				10 27				1 51					5 31		7 32		8 11	

A.—Stops at Lisfannon Halt when requested.

No. 19.—Empty Stock Train will run at 10 p.m., Buncrana to Pennyburn, Saturdays only.

daily goods. The heavy Buncrana service continued into the autumn of 1948, when it was reduced to two goods trains, the final shadowy remnant of former glories.

It must of course be added that market days and fairs (weekly at Carndonagh and Letterkenny as well as at Derry, and monthly at Churchill, Creeslough, Falcarragh, Dungloe and Crolly) brought momentary traffic peaks, cattle specials not being uncommon, and Sunday excursions from Derry were an established feature both of Derry life and of railway operating. In April 1923, Henry Hunt wrote in a preface to the pocket public timetable:

A special feature is being made this summer of the SUNDAY EXCURSIONS, which provide an opportunity for relaxation and pleasure for many. Very Reduced Fares are offered to promoters guaranteeing a minimum of 300 passengers, and arrangements are in operation which provide a substantial profit to promoters. The most popular trips run to Kilmacrenan (for Doon Well), Buncrana and Bally-liffin, the last named having the finest strand in Ireland. The Company's Steamboat 'Lake of Shadows' (which has been renovated, completed, and fitted with modern life-saving equipment, etc.) will be available on Sundays for guaranteed excursions to Rathmullan, or for the GRAND EVENING CRUISE ON LOUGH SWILLY. At the time of going to print (28th April) there are a few Sundays at the end of the Season vacant for this trip, but owing to the success which has attended this venture it is really unnecessary to advertise it, except to remind excursion promoters that the scenery and sandy shores of the Swilly are immeasurably superior to the Foyle for Excursion purposes, and an Excursion down the Swilly is cheaper and assures a greater profit to promoters than a similar Steamboat Excursion down the Foyle. *No Alcoholic Liquors* will be allowed on these Boat Excursions, but a Tea Buffet will be available to excursionists. Most of the Excursions will be accompanied, if not promoted, by a Band.

OPERATING

The entire system was single tracked, apart from the passing places and yards. At first the line was adequately worked on the principle of one engine in steam. Some form of signalling appears to have been in use at the intermediate stations to stop trains: thus in May 1875 Burnfoot was 'a flag station during the stay of the Presbyterian Synod'.

In 1887 the firm of McKenzie & Holland erected signals, and staff working was introduced with three sections: Pennyburn—Tooban, Tooban—Buncrana, and Tooban—Letterkenny. When one train was followed by another, the last carriage of the first carried an appropriate tail board.

By 1891 the staff system was being overwhelmed by the increasing traffic. The enquiry into the head-on collision at Springtown, near Derry, revealed that staffs were carried by regular trains, not specials. According to the station-master at Graving Dock: 'The staff-key is carried by the engine which works the sidings, and if there is more than one engine under steam, one goes without the staff-key'. The outcome of this accident was not only the introduction of a block telegraph and staff and ticket system (block sections being Pennyburn—Bridge End, Bridge End—Tooban, Tooban—Buncrana, Tooban—Newtoncunningham, Newtoncunningham—Letterkenny) but also of continuous automatic vacuum brakes.

After ten years of staff and ticket working, the Carndonagh line was opened, and being under the aegis of the Board of Works, it was provided with the Electric Train Staff, with Clonmany as an intermediate block post. The Burtonport Extension was also equipped with the E.T.S., with passing places at Creeslough and Gweedore, giving sections between Letterkenny and Burtonport of 20½, 17½ and 11½ miles. A block post at Kilmacrenan between Letterkenny and Creeslough was added about 1910. It was not long, however, before neglect of the E.T.S. installations reduced them to uselessness, as Tatlow soon discovered.

In 1909 the former Letterkenny Railway was equipped with E.T.S. This left only Derry—Tooban—Buncrana sections working with staff and ticket. On the L & LS part of the system between Tooban and Buncrana, Fahan was a block post from about 1918

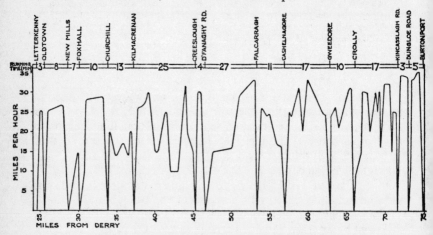

Speeds on the Burtonport Extension—a graph by E. Maslin, 1917

until shortly after the reorganisation of the railway working in April 1931, and again from May 1942 until September 1948.

The signalling introduced in 1887, and extended in 1901 and 1903 on the Carndonagh and Burtonport lines, was confined to the passing places and termini, and these had the usual starting, home and distants. Open ground frames were in use at the start, but after Tatlow's investigation, they were enclosed in wooden cabins. The Tooban signals were worked from a high cabin on a brick base.

To stop trains at conditional halts, crude semaphore signals were used, and were controlled either by the halt keepers, or by the passengers themselves, as at Lisfannon Links and Gallagh Road. Home-made board signals, which were caused to turn through 90° by chains connected to the heel of the crossing gates, were in use in the up direction at Pennyburn (where the board was diamond-shaped) and in the down directions at the next level crossing (round board) and at Gallagh Road (diamond). Painted red with a white border, they exhibited a red lamp at night.

Permanent speed restrictions were in force at the following places:

Between Graving Dock station and Pennyburn .... 8 m.p.h.
Through Tooban Junction; over the Swilly Bridge, between Pluck and Letterkenny; negotiating the 'S' curve at Farland Bank; approaching and over Owencarrow Viaduct; approaching crossing stations .... 10 m.p.h.

Beginning under Hunt's managership, the departure times of all trains were telegraphed to the manager's office at Pennyburn from the principal stations. There was a reciprocal arrangement between the Donegal and the Swilly stations in Letterkenny, so that passengers could make connections by up to five minutes detention. To get a quicker turn-round of rolling stock, Hunt appointed four district stock controllers, at Derry, Buncrana, Letterkenny and Burtonport.

Maximum load figures were laid down for the various sections of the line, but in practice the loads were often exceeded. The 1920 Appendix to the working timetable laid them down in the number of vehicles:

Engine Nos.	1—4	5—6	7, 8	9, 10	11, 12	13, 14	15, 16	17
Derry—Buncrana	15	24	20	15	24	20	20	15
Buncrana—Derry	16	24	22	16	24	22	22	15
Letterkenny line	12	17	14	12	17	16	14	12
B'port Extension	12	16	13	11	15	14	13	11
Carn. Extension	12	17	13	12	16	14	13	12

The route—especially to Burtonport—abounded in level-crossing gates. They were identified in four series (excluding gates at stations): Swilly Section, Nos 1-3 (plus the Pennyburn Gates); Carndonagh Section, Nos 1-15; Letterkenny Section, Nos 1-3; Burtonport Section, Nos 1-24.

The timetables became most complex in the early 1920s. The working timetable of 3 May 1920, and the relevant wagon workings are given below, the former in abbreviated form:

Train No.	1	20	2 Gds.	21 Gds.	3	22	4 S.O.	5 S.E.	23	6	7	8 S.O.
Londonderry	7.15	7.30	9.40	11.50	12.20	12.35	2.30	3.25	5.00	5.30	6.40	10.00
Buncrana	8.20		10.25		1.15		3.15	4.10		6.25	7.25	10.45
Carndonagh	9.40				2.35					7.36		
Letterkenny		9.05		4.40		2.23				6.55		
Burtonport		12.15		8.50						10.00		

Train No.	9	24 W.O.	10	11	25	12	13 L.E.	14 S.O.	15	26 Gds.	27	16 Gds
Burtonport					8.20		(a)			12.20	3.20	(b)
Letterkenny		7.20			11.50					4.35	6.55	
Carndonagh	7.00					11.45			4.09			
Buncrana	8.25		8.50	10.50		1.20	4.15	3.30	5.25			8.30
Londonderry	9.00	9.15	9.35	11.35	1.20	2.05	4.50	4.15	6.12	6.20	8.20	9.20

NOTES. (a) On Saturdays ran as No 18 (L.E.) and left Buncrana at 11.00 p.m.
(b) On Thursdays and Saturdays ran as passenger train (No 17) and arrived at Derry at 9.15 p.m.

WAGON WORKING ARRANGEMENTS

Train No.   *Down Trains*

1, goods in through vehicles for Carndonagh line.

2, goods for all stations, and work pull-out wagons to Buncrana.

3, through wagons for Buncrana and Carndonagh line stations.

4, through wagons for Buncrana only.

5, through wagons for Fahan and Buncrana.

6, bogie wagon containing shirt and bread traffic and through wagons for Clonmany and Carndonagh.

7, 8, through wagons for Buncrana.

20, up to 10 through wagons for 4 stations on Burtonport line. No pull-out wagons except goods booked at passenger train rates, must not attach vehicles at any intermediate station between Derry and Burtonport without special instructions.

21, traffic to and on the Burtonport line.

22, all traffic for stations Carrowen—Letterkenny, make up full load if necessary with Burtonport line wagons.

23, bread traffic for Burtonport line. May if necessary have load made up at Derry with wagons for any 2 of the following stations only: Churchill, Creeslough, Falcarragh, Dungloe and Burtonport. Must not attach vehicles at any station between Derry and Burtonport without special authority.

Up Trains

9, traffic in through vehicles from Carndonagh and live stock from intermediate stations. Bogie wagon will be attached at Carndonagh and shirt traffic will be taken forward in same from stations between Carndonagh and Buncrana.

10, perishable and live stock traffic only.

11, wagons as necessary Buncrana line to Derry.

12, goods traffic from intermediate stations to Buncrana, but will convey passenger and perishable traffic only Buncrana to Derry, and must run to time.

14, wagons from Buncrana, Fahan and Inch Road.

15, traffic in through wagons from Carndonagh, Clonmany, Drumfries and Ballymagan.

16, all goods traffic from intermediate stations.

24, goods between Letterkenny and Derry and intermediate stations. Must run to time and cross No. 20 at Newton.

25, full load goods for Derry in through wagons from any two stations en route.

26, perishable goods and live stock between all stations, Burtonport to Derry, and will work stock to and from intermediate stations on the Burtonport line. Two empty wagons for roadside traffic, one Burtonport to Derry, and one Burtonport to Letterkenny, must be put on this train at Burtonport. Stations having wagons for Letterkenny and Derry must marshal wagons so that Letterkenny wagons are in front of Derry wagons.

27, perishables, live stock, and important traffic only from all stations, Burtonport to Derry.

On all these trains, fish traffic to have preference. Creeslough, Cashelnagore and Kincasslagh must advise Burtonport by wire if there is any fish to attach, so that guards may be instructed not to attach vehicles at other stations.

ACCIDENTS

As on the County Donegal Railway, the most remarkable feature of the accidents on the Swilly's line was the many derailments caused by high winds. The whole of the Donegal coast lies open to the full force of the Atlantic gales, and in the bleak and treeless districts north and west of Letterkenny, difficulty and danger attended train working in the worst weather. Wind affected the other three narrow-gauge lines in the West of Ireland (the Tralee & Dingle, West Clare and Donegal lines), but the Swilly had more than its share.

The first trouble occurred seven months after the start of narrow-gauge operation. On 25 January 1884, with the barometer at 27.8 in.

the 4.50 p.m. mixed from Tooban to Letterkenny was crawling over the exposed embankment leading to the bridge over the River Swilly beyond Pluck station when all vehicles except the engine were derailed. None of the 11 passengers was injured. The railway had no breakdown crane, so they laid rails on the public road and dragged the derailed stock by horse power to Letterkenny.

Only 15 minutes before the blow-off, a similar accident occurred on the West Donegal at the west end of Stranorlar station. Both accidents were investigated by Major-General C. S. Hutchinson, who made the point that the stability of the narrow-gauge vehicles was adversely affected by their length, which he felt should not exceed 18 ft. The six-wheeled carriages then in use were 31 ft long. Neither Company took the General's advice; in fact both went on in later years to use still longer bogie stock.

The next derailment took place a few years after the opening of the Burtonport Extension. On 22 February 1906, a cross wind lifted two carriages as a train was crossing the Owencarrow Viaduct. The vehicles were held on the viaduct by the iron railing, and no-one was hurt, though ghoulish remarks were passed on the damaged railing for many years.

To add to the numerous difficulties of 1922, on Christmas Day two carriages of the mid-day down train were blown off the line at Dunfanaghy Road. Six weeks later, early on 7 February 1923, bad weather came in from the west and hurricane-force winds ripped over the Rosses, where there was scarcely a bush for shelter. The first train out of Burtonport left at 8.30 a.m. with three passengers. Near milepost 68¾, between Kincasslagh and Crolly, the train was on a falling grade on an 8 ft embankment above the surrounding rock and bog when a tremendous gust lifted three of the four vehicles and tipped them down the bank. Only the third brake van was left on the rails, separated from the engine by a gap of 100 ft. The shaken passengers were assisted to shelter in the van, while the driver went on light engine to Crolly to summon help. By the time he returned, another great gust had swept the line clear.

Reference has already been made to the worst of the blow-offs on the Owencarrow Viaduct on Friday, 30 January 1925. The 5.15 p.m. from Derry to Burtonport was made up of engine No. 14, one of the Hawthorn, Leslie 4—6—2 tanks, drawing covered wagon No. 55S, six-wheeled carriage No. 12S, bogie carriage No. 11B and combined carriage and van No. 8B. The train left Kilmacrenan at 7.52 p.m. with 14 passengers and would have been on the viaduct about 8.0 p.m.

Driver Robert McGuinness's statement tells what ensued:

> After travelling about 60 yards [over the viaduct] I again looked
> back and, seeing the side lights of the Guard's van, considered that
> everything was right. The wind was gusty and I was proceeding at the
> ordinary reduced speed and at the moment when I found it necessary
> to reach over to the regulator in order to maintain this speed I again
> cast another glance back, and then noticed that Carriage No. 12 was
> off the line and raised in the air. I at once applied the full force of the
> brake and pulled up almost immediately. At that time, carriage No. 12
> struck the wagon between it and the engine also sideways to the
> parapet.

John Hannigan the fireman, aged 25, said:

> The first thing I noticed was the first carriage seeming to rise from
> the rails. At that moment the driver, having also noticed something
> wrong, applied his brakes and brought the train to a standstill. I
> walked over to the other side and looked out and I said to the Driver,
> 'There is harm done tonight'. I got down first and he got down after
> me. He walked back to the van and got the guard out. When I was
> halfways over there was a woman coming crawling up the bank so I
> stopped and caught her hand and brought her to safety. Then there
> came three more up after that. They came up themselves.

The derailment happened above the embankment of granite
boulders between the girder and the masonry parts of the viaduct.
In the gloom the train men could see that behind the six-wheeler,
No. 11 was clear of the track and lying on its side at the top of the
slope, while No. 8 was resting on the damaged bridge parapet. The
six-wheeler was upside down, and wedged in mid-air between the
first of the masonry arches and the bank, its leading end crushed in.
The impact had brought away the complete roof, and all within the
carriage dropped to the rocks below them and were further injured
by boulders dislodged by the disturbance. Four passengers were
killed and four more injured.

Profiting by this hard-earned experience, the Swilly ballasted all
the carriages used on the Burtonport line, and purchased for this
280 slabs of cast iron, each weighing 1 cwt; one was put in the
the corners of each compartment. The Government suggested that
two anemometers should be erected to control traffic during storms.
The Company declined to have one on the viaduct as this would
have involved a semi-resident staff, but one was erected on an exposed site at Dunfanaghy Road station. The readings were regularly
sent to the Air Ministry, and in January 1927 the gauge justified its
existence by clocking a gust of 112 m.p.h.

Apart from these blow-offs, the line had the usual run of minor incidents. Derailments were usually linked with the condition of the permanent way, and for a time between 1905 and 1910 they were common on the Letterkenny section where the rails were lighter than on the rest of the system—originally 40 lb. per yd, but after 25 years of use worn down to 36-38 lb. At that time the heavy 4—8—0 and 4—8—4T engines were only permitted to run over the Letterkenny road in an emergency and at reduced speeds.

In a different category was the head-on collision on Sunday 21 June 1891 at Springtown, 1¼ miles from Derry, between a Derry—Letterkenny troop special and an empty train which had been improperly started from Tooban. This accident has already been mentioned in connection with the train staff working. The inspecting officer's report characteristically gives interesting detail of the make-up of the two trains and of the rather haphazard operating methods in force up to that time.

The special was hauled by No. 5 engine, bunker-first, followed by 'two waggons loaded with baggage, a waggon conveying a horse, seven carriages, a brake van, and two waggons of light luggage, 13 vehicles in all, in the order given, the brake-power consisting of a hand-brake for the four coupled wheels of the engine, and another hand-brake for the brake van, in which there was a guard'. There were between 250 and 300 militiamen on board, 14 of whom were injured. The engine crew jumped for their lives.

The empty train, a brake van and two carriages headed by No. 2 *Donegal* running bunker-first, was in the section as the result of the negligence of a number of people who should have known better, including the engine crew who were killed and the Tooban signal-man who could neither read nor write and who was understandably vague about the running of the special. As he said in the Assize Court, before his dismissal, 'When a written message is sent me, I get different persons to read it, sometimes passengers and sometimes men belonging to the road.' Asked who read the message given him on that fatal Sunday, he said, 'Dan Doherty, a neighbour; he could not make out something at the bottom, and then I got Mary Ann Quigley to read it. There was some part she could not make out. I went to no one after that.' Truly the management had much to contend with.

CHAPTER XIII

The Locomotives

STANDARD-GAUGE ENGINES

Six 5 ft 3 in.-gauge engines, two each of three classes, were used by the Swilly.

Nos. 1 and 2 were ordered on the recommendation of Sir John Macneill from Messrs Fossick & Hackworth of Stockton. Their construction was sub-contracted to the firm of Gilkes, Wilson & Co. of Middlesborough, and they bore this firm's works numbers (141-2). The difficulty which the Company experienced in paying for them has been referred to in Chapter II. They were six-coupled, side-tank engines with outside cylinders, 4 ft driving wheels and a wheelbase of 11 ft 6 in. The tanks held 800 gallons and the total weight in working order was 26 tons. The engines were characterised by low-pitched boilers, high chimneys with splayed caps, a high dome with safety-valve on the middle ring of the boiler, and a short straight weatherboard. Both were probably hired to McCormick when he was making the line to Farland.

No. 1 remained on the Swilly until the 1885 re-gauging rendered it obsolete, when it was sold, probably in September 1888. After the arrival of the next pair of engines and the relegation of the Farland branch, the Board seem to have decided to use No. 2 as a source of income, hiring it to the Belfast Central Railway in 1868. It remained away during the lean years around 1870-3, but returned in 1874. By the time it came back, the vacant number had been taken up, and it was renumbered 3. It was finally sold in 1882 to an unknown purchaser. No sketches or photographs of the Fossick & Hackworth engines are known to exist.

After the Fossick & Hackworth engines came two products of the Newcastle works of Messrs Robert Stephenson (makers' Nos. 1609-10). They were six-coupled, saddle-tank, inside-cylinder engines, with 3 ft 6 in. driving wheels and a wheelbase of 10 ft. The tanks were square, they had stove-pipe chimneys and domes over the

LIST OF 5 ft 3 in. GAUGE LOCOMOTIVES

No.	Date	Builder/Builder's No.	Type	Cyls. (in.)	Wheel Diam.	Wheel Base	Weight (Tons)	Remarks
1	1862	Fossick & Hackworth (Gilkes, Wilson & Co.) (141)	0.6.0T	13 x 24 (o)	4' 0"	11' 6"	26	Sold 1888 for scrap. 800 gallon tanks
2/3	1862	Fossick & Hackworth (Gilkes, Wilson & Co.) (142)	0.6.0T	13 x 24 (o)	4' 0"	11' 6"	26	Hired to Belfast Central Rly 1868. Renumbered in 1874. Sold 1885 to unknown. 800 gallon tanks
3	1864	R. Stephenson & Co. (1609)	0.6.0ST	13 x 20 (i)	3' 6"	10' 0"		Hired LPHC 1865-9, sold LPHC 1869, sold McC & McF 1883, scr. c. 1889. 570 gall tank, 7 cwt coal
4/2	1864	R. Stephenson & Co. (1610)	0.6.0ST	13 x 20 (i)	3' 6"	10' 0"		Renumbered in 1868. Sold to Derry Harbour Comm. in 1883. Scrapped in 1891. 570 gallon tanks. 7 cwt coal
4	1876	Sharp, Stewart & Co. (2645)	0.6.0T	15 x 22 (i)	4' 6"	12' 3"	31	Named St Patrick. Sold to Cork & Bandon Rly in 1885 (their No. 14). 650 gallon tanks
5	1879	Sharp, Stewart & Co. (2836)	0.6.0T	15 x 22 (i)	4' 6"	12' 3"	31	Named St Columb. Sold to Cork & Bandon Rly in 1885 (their No. 15). 650 gallon tanks

Notes: 1. The names of the Sharp, Stewart engines are as given in *The Narrow Gauge Railways of Ireland* (Fayle) and in the *Journal of the Irish Railway Record Society*, **4**, 255. The records of R. Stephenson & Co. state that their Nos. 1609 and 1610 were, respectively, supplied as *John Cooke* and *St Columb*.

2. Additional dimensions of Stephenson engines: boiler, 3 ft 1 in. x 11 ft 3 in.; boiler c/l, 5 ft 3 in.; grate. 7.0 sq. ft; heating surface, 41½ + 495½ sq. ft; tubes, 74 x 2 in. diam. (J.I.R.R.S., **4**, 255).

3. Additional dimensions of Sharp, Stewart engines: wheelbase, 5 ft 11½ in. x 6 ft 3½ in.; grate, 12 sq. ft; heating surface, 70 + 850 sq. ft; tubes, 200 x 1¾ in. diam. (J.I.R.R.S., **4**, 255).

fireboxes. Coal was kept in bunkers at the rear, and the crews reached the cabs over the rear buffer beams, being protected in front by plain weather boards. They had a horn in place of a whistle, and were colloquially known in Derry as 'the Coffee Pots'.

The first (No. 3) arrived in September 1864. During the next year it was hired to the Londonderry Port & Harbour Commissioners, who after four years bought it. It had 19 years around the quays, and 5 years with McCrea & McFarland. The second engine (No. 4) was delivered in October 1864, and was renumbered 2 in 1868. It remained with the Swilly for 19 years and was then bought by the Harbour Commissioners to take the place of its twin. It was scrapped in 1891.

The last pair of standard-gauge engines were 0—6—0 side tanks by Sharp, Stewart. The first was ordered in 1876 after Ellis the locomotive superintendent had reported 'the present engines with repairs may last 10 or 12 years, but are not quite up to the present work—the fireboxes will not last more than 2 years'. So later that year delivery was made of No. 4, that number then being vacant, and the engine was named *St Patrick*. Three years later, its sister engine (No. 5) was taken into stock and named *St Columb*. John Cooke, Owner' was painted in small letters on the back buffer

Elevation of Sharp, Stewart 5 ft 3 in. gauge locomotive No. 4

beams as both were hired (see page 156). This pair of engines had larger coupled wheels than their predecessors, 4 ft 6 in diameter, and a wheelbase of 5 ft 11 in. x 6 ft 3½ in. The crew were protected by bent-over weather boards. Both machines worked on the Swilly

until re-gauging. They were auctioned on 7 May 1885, going to the
Cork & Bandon Railway, where they became 4—4—0T engines and
were scrapped in 1907 and 1921.

NARROW-GAUGE ENGINES 1885-1904

A total of 22 3 ft-gauge steam locomotives belonged to the L & LS.
They are listed in the table on page 146. The table on pages 148-149
gives the dimensions of each class. The average age of the engines
when scrapped was 44 years, two having the shortest lives of 27
years, and two sharing the distinction of living to 55. Only seven
were named, and of these only three carried names throughout.

Three 0—6—2T engines with inside frames were ordered by
McCrea & McFarland from Black, Hawthorn & Co., on the instructions of the Lough Swilly directors in 1882, to work from Tooban to
Letterkenny. As noted in Chapter III they were hire-purchased by
the railway. The first was obtained in 1882 and the contractors used
it for ballasting the Letterkenny line. It became No. 1 in the Swilly
stock and was named *J. T. Macky* after the then chairman. The
'Macky', as it was called, was hired to McCrea & McFarland for use
on their construction of the Glenties branch of the Donegal Railway
between 1891 and 1895. The minutes also record that it was
hired to McCrea for a few months in 1886 for use on the Clogher
Valley Railway contract. It was scrapped in 1911.

The second and third Black, Hawthorn engines came during 1883
and were named *Londonderry* (No. 2) and *Donegal* (No. 3). They
differed from *J. T. Macky* in having side tanks holding 600 gallons
of water, whereas the *Macky* held only 500 gallons, mainly in a
well tank, and partly in short side tanks. The cab of No. 1 was
completely enclosed, Nos. 2 and 3 had cabs open at the back. The
name plates of all three were large cast brass affairs, with letters
about 6 in. high. On No. 1 the plates were on the front ring of the
boiler, on Nos. 2 and 3 they were fixed to the middle of the side
tanks. Nos. 2 and 3 were scrapped in 1912 and 1913.

When the Derry—Buncrana line was re-gauged in early 1885,
Black, Hawthorn supplied a fourth engine (No. 4), an 0—6—0 side-
tank type with the name on a combined number/name plate. The
rigid wheel-base of 11 ft 6 in was found to be tight on curves
and about 1902 the leading part of the side rods was removed,
making it a 2—4—0T, perhaps before the Swilly's general
adoption of having thin flanges on the driving wheels. Initially
the cab was open at the back, as on Nos. 2 and 3, but it was later

enclosed. The boiler was larger than on the previous engines, but no details have survived of the dimensions. At first, Salter-type safety valves on the dome were used, but later a large, flat-topped dome was fitted at reboilering and Ramsbottom safety valves placed on the firebox. About 1913 it was renumbered 17 and the name was removed at the same time. (Mr R. N. Clements is of the opinion it was numbered 4A in 1912-4, a possible preliminary to scrapping, followed by reprieve and reboilering.) It was sold for scrap in 1940.

In 1885 McCrea & McFarland bought two Stephenson engines at the sale of the Glenariff Railway in Co. Antrim. They shipped them to Derry and, after two years hiring, the Swilly purchased them in 1887. They were the first 3 ft-gauge engines in Ireland. Both were 2—4—0 side tanks, with Bissel trucks and outside cylinders. On arrival on the Swilly, they became No. 5 and No. 6. Little evidence exists of how they performed, but their short career of 14 years suggests that they were in poor order when acquired.

No. 6 was derailed near Fahan on 17 September 1889 because of a missing length of rail (see p.45). No. 5 was withdrawn in 1899, but its fellow, numbered 6A lay derelict until about 1904 though still on the stock list. By this time a weather board, fitted in 1888, had been removed from No. 6A.

The advisability of having stronger engines for the hilly Carndonagh Extension was advocated by F. G. Miller, and with the approval of the Board of Works an order was placed in 1899 with Hudswell, Clarke of Leeds for a pair of 4—6—2T engines costing £1,850 each. This wheel arrangement was to become popular on the Swilly, the only Irish Company to have it. The two newcomers took up the now vacant Nos. 5 and 6. When delays became frequent to trains on the Letterkenny line due to the poor state of the old engines, the Swilly could not resist sending them there The Board of Works complained about this misuse of machines specifically bought for the Carndonagh Extension and in December 1899 took legal proceedings.

No. 5 was renumbered 15 in 1913. The locomotive superintendent's reports mention that it had a broken eccentric rod on 14 February 1920, and failed near Derry on 1 June 1920 with a broken eccentric strap. A broken eccentric rod again caused a failure at Clonmany on 26 October 1923. In April 1923, a new boiler, built by Hudswell, Clarke, was fitted. The firebox was originally of the round top type, but sometime after 1945 the engine was given a Belpaire box. It worked the last train into Derry on 8 August 1953,

L

LIST OF 3 ft 0 in. GAUGE LOCOMOTIVES

No.	Date	Builder/Builder's No.		Type	Name	Remarks	Scrapped
1	1882	Black, Hawthorn & Co.	(684)	0.6.2T	*J. T. Macky*	Water mainly in well tank. Cab enclosed	1911
2	1883	do.	(742)	0.6.2T	*Londonderry*	Cab open at back	1912
3	1883	do.	(743)	0.6.2T	*Donegal*	Cab open at back	1913
4/17	1885	do.	(834)	0.6.0T	*Innishowen*	Renumbered 1913. Name removed 1914	1940
5/5A	1885	R. Stephenson & Co.	(2088)	2.4.0T		Built 1873, ex-Glenariff L & D Co.	1899
6/6A	1885	do.	(2089)	2.4.0T		Built 1873, ex-Glenariff L & D Co.	1904
5/15	1899	Hudswell, Clarke & Co.	(518)	4.6.2T		Cost £1,850. Belpaire firebox latterly. Reno. 1913	1954
6/16	1899	do.	(519)	4.6.2T		Cost £1,850. Reno. 1913	1953
7	1901	do.	(577)	4.6.2T	*Edward VII*	Cost £2,060. Named for Royal Train in 1903	1940
8	1901	A. Barclay, Sons & Co.	(562)	4.6.2T		Cost £2,060	1954
1	1902	do.	(933)	4.6.0T			1940
2	1902	do.	(934)	4.6.0T			1954
3	1902	do.	(935)	4.6.0T			1954
4	1902	do.	(936)	4.6.0T			1953
9	1904	Kerr, Stuart & Co.	(845)	4.6.2T	*Aberfoyle*	Name not carried throughout	1928
10	1904	do.	(846)	4.6.2T	*Richmond*	Name not carried throughout	1954
11	1905	Hudswell, Clarke & Co.	(746)	4.8.0		Cost £2,675. Belpaire firebox	1933
12	1905	do.	(747)	4.8.0		Cost £2,675. Belpaire firebox	1954
13	1910	Hawthorn, Leslie & Co.	(2801)	4.6.2T		Cost £2,050 (Scotter Award). Belpaire firebox	1940
14	1910	do.	(2802)	4.6.2T		Cost £2,050 (Scotter Award). Belpaire firebox	1943
5	1912	Hudswell, Clarke & Co.	(985)	4.8.4T		Cost £2,765. Belpaire firebox	1954
6	1912	do.	(986)	4.8.4T		Cost £2,765. Belpaire firebox	1954

and was scrapped in the summer of 1954. No. 6 became No. 16 in 1913 and seems to have escaped the eccentric troubles of its twin. It lay out of use for many years, was slowly cannibalised and finally scrapped during 1953.

In March and April 1901, Nos. 7 and 8, very similar to the 1899 pair, came from Hudswell, Clarke at a cost of £2,100. They differed from the earlier two in having Allan straight link motion in place of Stephenson motion, the only case where the former was used in Ireland. No. 7 was chosen to work a royal train in July 1903, and was repainted and named *Edward VII* for the occasion (Plate 64). The train conveyed Their Majesties King Edward VII and Queen Alexandra from Buncrana, where they landed at the pier, and took them to the site of the old Middle Quay station in Derry, a decorated platform being erected to receive them. A saloon coach for the royal guests was borrowed from the Ballymena & Larne section of the Belfast & Northern Counties Railway. No. 7 is known to have failed with a broken eccentric strap in September 1918, and to have had heavy repairs in late 1922, mid-1924, spring 1926 and early 1930. Ten years later it was scrapped. No. 8 remained in service until the line closed and was cut up in the spring of 1954.

For use on the Burtonport Extension four new engines were supplied to the specification of T. M. Batchen of the Board of Works. They were 4—6—0 side tanks, built in Kilmarnock by Andrew Barclay, Sons & Co., with outside bearings to the coupled wheels. In their general design they were similar to the six Neilson engines

Elevation of Nos. 1—4. Redrawn from maker's plans

supplied to the Donegal Railway in 1893, and to a Kerr, Stuart engine made for the West Clare Railway in 1903. Despite complaints that they were unsuited to the Burtonport road, the Barclay

LOCOMOTIVE DIMENSIONS. (3 ft 0 in. GAUGE)

Class	Cyls. (in.)	Wheel Diameter			Wheel Base
		L.W.	D.W.	T.W.	
Black, Hawthorn 0.6.2T (1882)*	13 x 19	—	3' 6"	2' 4½"	9' 3" fixed + 7' 7" = 16' 10"
Black, Hawthorn 0.6.2T (1883)*	13 x 19	—	3' 6"	2' 4½"	9' 3" fixed + 7' 7" = 16' 10"
Black, Hawthorn 0.6.0T (1885)	14 x 20	—	3' 6"	—	5' 9" + 5' 9" = 11' 6"
R. Stephenson 2.4.0T (pur. 1887)*	15 x 20	2' 6"	3' 9"	—	5' 6" + 6' 6" = 12' 0"
Hudswell, Clarke 4.6.2T (1899)	15 x 22	2' 3"	3' 9"	2' 6"	4' 7" + 3' 9½" + 2 (4' 6") + 5' 0" = 22' 4½"
Hudswell, Clarke 4.6.2T (1901)†	15 x 22	2' 3"	3' 9"	2' 6"	4' 7" + 3' 9½" + 2 (4' 6") + 5' 0" = 22' 4½"
Barclay 4.6.0T (1902)	14 x 20	2' 1"	3' 6"	—	4' 3" + 3' 7½" + 4' 2" + 5' 4" = 17' 4½"
Kerr, Stuart 4.6.2T (1904)	14 x 20	2' 0"	3' 6"	2' 3"	4' 6" + 3' 9½" + 2 (4' 6") + 4' 5" = 21' 8½"
Hudswell, Clarke 4.8.0 (1905)	15½ x 22	2' 1"	3' 9"	3' 0"‡	4' 7" + 3' 7½" + 3 (4' 6") = 21' 8½"
Hawthorn, Leslie 4.6.2T (1910)	14½ x 22	2' 1½"	3' 9"	2' 7"	4' 9" + 4' 0" + 2 (4' 6") + 5' 9" = 23' 6"
Hudswell, Clarke 4.8.4T (1912)	16 x 20	2' 1"	3' 9"	2' 1"	4' 6" + 4' 3" + 3 (4' 6") + 4' 3" + 4' 6" = 31' 0"

All dimensions except those marked * from LLSR diagram book.
† No. 15 with Belpaire firebox, heating surface 86 + 664 sq ft
‡ Tender

LOCOMOTIVE DIMENSIONS (3 ft 0 in. GAUGE)—continued

Class	Boiler Diam.	Length	C/Line	W.P. (lb.)	Tank Capacity (gall.)	Coal (tons)	Grate Area (ft.²)	Heating Surface (ft.²) F/Box	Tubes	Total Weight (tons)
Black, Hawthorn 0.6.2T (1882)	3' 1"	10' 4"		140	500	1¼	8¾	49	543	24
Black, Hawthorn 0.6.2T (1883)	3' 1"	10' 4"		140	600	1¼	8¾	49	543	24
Black, Hawthorn 0.6.0T (1885)‡	3' 6⅜"	9' 2¾"	5' 3½"	150	650	1¼	8¾	53½	630	27
R. Stephenson 2.4.0T (pur. 1887)	3' 8"	10' 0"			600		10½	54	642½	26½
Hudswell, Clarke 4.6.2T (1899)	3' 9"	10' 0"	6' 2"	150	850	1¼	12½	80	700	41
Hudswell, Clarke 4.6.2T (1901)	3' 8"	10' 0"	6' 2"	{166 150‡	850	1¼	12½	76	701	41
Barclay 4.6.0T (1902)	3' 7"	9' 1⅜"	6' 1"	150	750	1¼	9½	63	565	30
Kerr, Stuart 4.6.2T (1904)	3' 4"	10' 3"	6' 0"	150	700	1	11	69	581	35
Hudswell, Clarke 4.8.0 (1905)	4' 0"	10' 6"	6' 3"	{170 160‡	1500*	4*	15	116	889	37 + 21½*
Hawthorn, Leslie 4.6.2T (1910)	4' 7"	10' 3"	6' 6"	{175 160‡	1300	1¾	11½	75	728	41½
Hudswell, Clarke 4.8.4T (1912)	4' 0"	10' 1"	6' 6"	{180 160‡	1500	2½	17	130	917	53¼†

* Tender
† Previously accepted as 51 tons
‡ Figures for second boiler

engines were in fact very reliable when given tasks within their power, and they were popular with their crews. They were numbered No. 1 to 4 in a separate Burtonport series, continuing thus until the practice of having two separate series of engines was ended in 1913. The first of the Burtonport Barclays to go was No. 1, scrapped in 1940. Nos. 2 and 3 were in use to the end, and were disposed of in 1954. Although No. 4 survived until autumn 1953, it was not much used latterly.

In 1904 two further 4—6—2T engines came, this time from Kerr, Stuart & Co. Referred to as the 'Letterkenny engines', they became Nos. 9 and 10 in the stock list. They were originally employed on Derry—Letterkenny trains, for which their limited coal and water capacity was no disadvantage, and were named *Aberfoyle* and *Richmond* after the homes of directors in Derry. The names seem to have been removed, perhaps during the first war, but one of

Elevation of No. 9

One of *Aberfoyle's* plates survived and for many years was on the gate of the house of that name in Londonderry. No. 9 was derelict by 1920, but escaped scrapping until 1927. No. 10 worked until the closure.

THE GIANTS AND OTHERS

Until 1905, Letterkenny and Burtonport were coaling points for engines working on the Extension. In order to work the full double journey without taking coal, two noteworthy 4—8—0 engines were designed by Mr Conner. They were the first engines in Ireland to have eight-coupled wheels, the first on the Swilly with Belpaire fireboxes and Walschaerts valve gear, and the only tender engines ever to work on an Irish narrow-gauge line. Although their weight was 37 tons, their wheel arrangement gave them the low axle loading of

6 tons 12 cwt. The tenders ran on six wheels, and with 4 tons of coal and 1,500 gallons of water they weighed 21 tons 3 cwt. They came in December 1905 from Messrs Hudswell, Clarke of Leeds, cost £2,750 each, and were numbered 11 and 12 in the Swilly stock. The same firm also supplied a spare boiler, given in November 1921 to No. 11, which also underwent heavy repairs in May 1924 and November 1925; between these dates a slide bar bolt broke, disabling the engine on the Letterkenny road. Early in its career, No. 11's tender drawbar broke on the Letterkenny line and the driver sustained fatal injuries. This engine was the first to go, being scrapped in 1933, after lying idle for five years.

No. 12 was slightly damaged on 11 February 1921 by a malicious derailment near Creeslough. The engine is known to have been shopped for heavy repairs in July 1923, August 1926 and March 1928, and was given a repaired spare boiler in the spring of 1925. During the 1930s, No. 11 was cannibalised to keep No. 12 working, the latter continuing on the Burtonport line until the closure. After hauling the demolition trains during the lifting of the Extension, it was relegated to Letterkenny shed and did not work again, being finally sold for scrap to a Belfast firm in the autumn of 1953.

The Scotter Award allowed the Company to buy two more engines in 1910. They reverted to the 4—6—2T type, and placed the order with the Newcastle firm of Hawthorn, Leslie & Co. at a cost of £2,050 each; numbering them 13 and 14. Originally in L &LS stock, they were transferred to LBE stock in exchange for Nos. 5 and 6. Of the four lots of 4—6—2T engines used by the Swilly, the Hawthorns had by far the greatest water capacity, holding 1,300 gallons, compared to the 700 gallons of the two Kerr, Stuarts and the 900 gallons of the four Hudswell, Clarkes. The large tanks were obviously an attempt to obtain the advantages of the two tender engines, but they were unpopular with the men, who held that they rolled badly at speed, probably due to having too high a centre of gravity. No. 13 was damaged by a malicious derailment near Kincasslagh Road in 1921; from the superintendent's reports it seems to have had a history of frequent heavy repairs, and was scrapped in 1940. No. 14 was the engine involved in the Owencarrow Viaduct blow-off in January 1925. It was scrapped in 1943.

In September 1912, Hudswell Clarke delivered the last two engines of the Swilly's stock. They were a unique and impressive pair, the only 4—8—4T engines in the British Isles. With a tractive effort of 14,080 lb. at 75 per cent of their standard working pressure of 165 p.s.i., these massive engines were not only the most powerful ever put on Irish narrow-gauge lines, but when delivered had only slightly less tractive effort than the largest Irish standard-gauge engines. They were popular on the Swilly. The Company and the men were proud of them, and latterly maintained them in good order. As soon as they were built, they adorned the makers' catalogues, and continued to do so for at least 35 years. No. 5 appears from the records to have had a rather better repair record than its sister: heavy repairs to it are listed in early 1919, late 1923 and 1926, and in January 1929.

No. 6 had the distinction of being sent to the County Donegal's shops for general overhaul in 1917. A year or so earlier it blew a boiler tube at Clonmany one morning when Deeney senior was driving, and lay disabled there while, to quote another driver, 'the grass grew around her'. During that time much of the copper piping was stolen. Then, when the Irish Railway Executive Committee had decided that it should be repaired at Stranorlar, Hedley Connell with No. 7 towed it to Letterkenny, when the Donegal men took over. On 7 April 1917, Maslin wrote cheerfully to R. M. Livesey, the locomotive superintendent of the CDRJC: 'Although the engine is one of the larger types, it is one of the newest and requires least renewal'.

Livesey's report, dated 24 April, and covering 4½ pages of foolscap, tells a rather different story. Generally:

> The whole engine has evidence of gross neglect, everything about it was in a filthy state; very little or no attention had been paid to lubrication, even washing out of boiler appears to have been neglected, for the bottom of the firebox sides appear to be choked up solid with dirt; even a finger could not be inserted at washout doors owing to the amount of solid matter gathered there.

Two years after the Donegal had ministered to the needs of No. 6, the patched firebox was past repairing, and a new copper firebox was fitted to the boiler in June 1921 at the Great Northern works in Dundalk, while Pennyburn gave a heavy repair. Before the next heavy repair, in August 1924, the engine covered 65,000 miles. Like No. 5, it survived until the Swilly closed, though for the last year neither of those great engines moved beyond the confines of Pennyburn yard, for the decaying track was reckoned to be unsafe for them on scheduled trains. No. 5 was, however, out on the lifting train in late 1953, being the only type with big enough tanks. Both were offered for sale in running order, but they failed to find a purchaser, or even a museum home, and were cut up for scrap in 1954. Most published references to the Swilly's unique 4—8—4 tanks give their weight in working order as 51 tons. It now appears from the records of the builders (made available by Mr R. N. Redman, of Messrs Hudswell, Clarke Ltd.) that this weight was that of the original proposed design, and later this was modified by the Company to 42 tons 19 cwt 3 qr empty and 54 tons 16 cwt 3 qr in working order. In fact, the actual weight on the works balances in full working order was 58 tons 15 cwt 2 qr, which includes: water in boiler 3 tons 3 cwt 2 qr, water in tanks 6 tons 16 cwt, coal 2 tons, sand 8 cwt 2 qr. These figures are thus around 7¾ tons above those hitherto published.

In the companion volume, reference has been made to a request from the Swilly in September 1922 to the CDRJC for the loan of a 2—6—4 tank for a demonstration run to Burtonport. The Swilly or their manager apparently had in mind the purchase of several new engines, and felt that the Donegal's latest might suit them. The engines of this class carried 2½ tons of coal and 1,500 gallons of water, and unlike any of the Swilly engines were superheated. Forbes of the Donegal was patently not keen to oblige the Swilly, and his reply to Hunt on 3 October 1922 was a gem:

> I am afraid I have not sufficient authority to sanction the sending of one of our engines off our own line, particularly at present. If I were to take this authority on myself, it might happen that we would never get the engine back again, by a combination of circumstances in which the Irregulars of Burtonport and the bogs of Dungloe would play their respective parts, and as you are gifted with a lively imagination, I leave you to judge the figure I would cut in explaining this circumstance to my Directors.

So no Donegal engine traversed the length of the Burtonport line on an exhibition run, though many years later they did occasionally work Doon Well excursions to Kilmacrenan. The Swilly never bought any further engines, and we can now only speculate what they might have been had Hunt and his superintendent been given a free hand.

No data on the detailed workings of individual engines has been published, and it seems doubtful if any exists. During 1963 a collection of guards' report books covering the Carndonagh Extension on sample dates between 1919 and 1935 came to light. The principal points which emerge are: the four Barclay engines (Nos. 1-4) paid few visits to Carndonagh; the 4—8—4 tanks (Nos. 5 and 6) rarely appeared after 1920; the 1901 class (Nos. 7 and 8) saw much service on the Extension; there is no record of Nos. 9, 10, 14 and 17 being used, although it is known that Nos. 9 and 10 worked the 8.0 a.m.

market special from Derry to Carndonagh on Mondays; understandably the 4—8—0 engines rarely reached Carndonagh, being particularly suited to the longer Burtonport line; and Nos. 15 and 16 were the most frequent performers, fully meriting their nickname of 'the Carn engines'.

ENGINE LIVERIES

Nothing reliable is known of the colour of the standard-gauge engines.

The earliest livery of the narrow-gauge engines appears to have been 'a bright grass green', lined with black with an edging of white. Presumably the buffer beams were vermilion, and early photographs show a thin edging of white. The smokebox and chimneys were apparently black. The four Black, Hawthorn engines had cast brass number plates: No. 1 on the bunker sides, Nos. 2 and 3 on the tanks and No. 4 combined with the nameplate. The Glenariffs had their numbers painted on the tanks. A number painted on the bunker back sheet was also in vogue for a time.

The records of Messrs Hudswell, Clarke specify 'pea green' as the main colour, and after lining in black and white, this livery was finished with three coats of best engine copal varnish. By 1912, when this firm built the 4—8—4 tanks, the buffer beams were to be vermilion varnished with road numbers in 6 in. gold letters'; then the Swilly hurriedly economised, and asked for yellow letters. The outside of the engine frames was to be chocolate, lined with red, with the inside and the frame stays vermilion. The smokebox, chimney and saddle casting were to be given two coats of dull black, the wheels were to have green centres and black tyres. The side tanks were lettered L & LSR, or in the case of the 4—6—0 and the 4—8—4 tanks, L & BER.

Probably about the time of the First World War, as engines came through the shops they were repainted black and were either lined in red or left unlined. Photographs of engines in this livery indicate that, for a time at least, some of them were not lettered. This black livery persisted on more than half of the engine stock until they were scrapped, but in later years they began to show a charming variety in lining colours. Thus, Mr H. S. Irvine recorded the following variants in the spring of 1948: No. 3, black, lined green; No. 4, black, lined yellow (for a time this had '4' on the side of the bunker); No. 8, black, lined red and green; No. 12, black, unlined and unlettered, and with red coupling rods lined in yellow; No. 16, black, lined red.

By the thirties, the numbers were painted in yellow on the right side of the vermilion buffer beams, with the prefix 'No.' on the left side. The four 8-coupled engines all carried their numbers in relief on large oval plates, which in the case of Nos. 5 and 6 also bore the maker's name; these plates were placed on the bunker sides of the tank engines, and on the cab sides of the tender engines.

During the thirties, reversion to a green livery began, but the shade which was chosen, particularly for No. 10, was distinctly darker than the original. Variety was still present: in 1948 No. 2 was recorded as lined in yellow and black, Nos. 5 and 6 were lined in yellow with green side rods, while No. 10 was unlined, apart from red side rods lined in yellow. During this period some of the engine tanks carried a diamond-shaped outline containing the letters 'L.S.R.', which were elaborately serified, and resembled a monogram.

CHAPTER XIV

Carriages and Wagons

STANDARD-GAUGE STOCK

Reference has been made in Chapter II to the earliest order for carriages and wagons, placed with Fossick & Hackworth in February 1863. This gave the Company two first/second composites, two thirds, one goods brake van, four flat and four covered wagons. It seems likely that, as with the two engines, Fossick & Hackworth subcontracted them to the Cheltenham firm of Shackleford. Payment proved to be difficult, but a Derry businessman, John Cooke, came to the rescue and hired the vehicles to the railway. They had six wheels; the composites had four compartments, arranged 2112, and the thirds had five compartments.

The modest supply of wagons soon proved to be inadequate. In July 1863 it was arranged that, on the Board's behalf. McCormick the contractor would order 12 ballast wagons from the Ashbury Railway Carriage & Iron Co. at a cost of £834. He was to hire them while ballasting the line, after which they were apparently used by the Swilly as flat or open wagons. With these, the total of flat wagons should have been 16, but the first recorded stock list, in 1868, gives only 12 flats, but four cattle wagons as well. Probably four of the flats were rebuilt locally as cattle wagons, which would have been the unroofed type then common.

The increase in numbers, and the ownership of the standard-gauge rolling stock, is summarised in the table overleaf, which is abstracted from the half-yearly reports (hired vehicles are bracketed).

The next mention in the minute book of an addition to the rolling stock is on 23 February 1869, when a tender was considered from Thomas Firth & Son of Belfast for six wagons (£100 each), one third brake (£200) and one goods van at £107. The Company ordered only the third brake, but asked as well for one third-class carriage at a cost of £215. As this was required to be 'same style as last but two feet longer and to carry about 60 passengers', these cannot have been the first acquisitions from Firth & Son; moreover it has been stated that five ex-Firth thirds came up for sale at the 1885 auction. The Firth carriages were four-wheelers, and open inside.

Year	Carriages				
	1st	2nd	3rd	1st/2nd	Total
1863	—	—	2	2	4
1864	—	—	2	2	4
1868	—	—	2 (2)	2	6
1869	—	—	2 (3)	2	7
1872	1	2	—(5)	1	9
1874	2 (1)	2	2 (5)	—	12
1878	—(1)	—(5)	2 (5)	2	15
1884	—(1)	—(5)	2 (5)	2	15

Year	Wagons				
	B/Vans	Flat	Covered	Cattle	Total
1863	1	4	4	—	9
1864	1	16	4	—	21
1868	1	12	4	4	21
1869	1 (1)	12	4	4	22
1872	1 (1)	12 (3)	4	4	25
1874	1 (1)	12 (5)	4 (6)	4	33
1878	1 (1)	12 (7)	4 (10)	4	39
1884	1 (1)	12 (7)	4 (10)	4	39

At some later date, three six-wheeled carriages came from the Metropolitan Carriage & Wagon Co. Ltd. Untraceable in the minute books, they were probably a single four-compartment first and two five-compartment seconds. Since two seconds and one first are shown in the 1872 stock list, it might at first seem that these are the Metropolitan vehicles, but the half-yearly report states that the first was a converted composite, and the seconds conversions from older thirds. The absence of composite carriages in the 1874 totals suggests that both of the Shacklefords were made into firsts in the Derry shops, and their reappearance in the 1878 list may indicate a reversal of the process when traffic demanded it. The Metropolitan carriages most likely came around 1878, and were actually owned by John Cooke; after the 1885 re-gauging they went to the Cork & Bandon Railway.

That more detailed records of the standard-gauge stock do not appear to exist is no doubt largely because vehicles were only hired by the Company. No drawings, photographs or descriptions of their livery are known.

Classification of the narrow-gauge carriage and wagon stock is complicated by the fact that separately numbered vehicles were maintained for the L & BE. The duplicate numbering persisted even after it had been dropped for the engine stock in 1913.

The earliest extant official census of rolling stock is dated 1925, and while it takes account of the L & LS and L & BE series, it does not record any earlier withdrawals, scrappings, or renumberings. It shows that at that time six separate series of numbers existed:

L & LS stock:	Carriages	Nos. 1-35
	Brake vans	Nos. 1-5 (plus six others numbered in the wagon list)
	Timber trucks	Nos. 1-3
	Wagons	Nos. 1-196
L & BE stock:	Carriages	Nos. 1-13
	Wagons	Nos. 1-91

There were also six tank wagons owned by the B.P. and Anglo-American oil companies, which were numbered separately from these series.

L & LS carriages. The first narrow-gauge carriages to come to the Swilly were twelve six-wheelers made by the Railway Carriage Co. Ltd., of Oldbury in 1884. Further instalments took the total up to 22 vehicles by 1899. All were of similar style, 31 ft 9 in long, with the three axles arranged on the Cleminson principle. This gave the carriages flexibility on sharp curves, as the outer axles were pivoted and connected to the centre axle by radius links, while the centre pair of wheels had considerable side-play.

So far as is known all these six-wheeled carriages had five compartments, partitioned to the roof and the same width for each class. The windows had square corners, and the footboards ran the full length of the vehicle. The side panels were later replaced with matchboarding, laid vertically. When the original sides were completely replaced the mouldings were stripped away, giving a flush-sided vehicle, as in the case of No. 12 after the Owencarrow derailment. None of these carriages had any luggage or brake compartments. They ran in trains with one of the passenger brake vans; vacuum brakes were not fitted until 1892.

The initial purchases in 1884-5 gave the Swilly 13 thirds and five first/second composites, a stock not increased until 1895. The 1925 census shows only three composites between Nos. 1 and 18, and omits Nos. 9, 14, 15 and 16. From the 1891 Springtown accident report, No. 9 is known to have been a third, so that of the missing Nos. 14-16, two must have been composites and one a third. Their fate is not known. In 1895, Nos. 19 and 20 were added to the stock, the latter being a tricomposite, or in Swilly parlance a 'trio'. In 1899 the last pair of six-wheelers came; initially both were composites, but after a fire on 28 February 1923, No. 22 was rebuilt as a third.

General Hutchinson's recommendation after the 1884 blow-off that carriages longer than 18 ft should not be used was never accepted. If it had been, the Swilly would have acquired a stud of four-wheelers. As it was, when buying for the opening of the Carndonagh line, the Company departed still further from the General's suggestion and obtained 14 bogie carriages (Nos. 23-35). These were 35 ft 9 in. long and were built by the Lancaster Railway Carriage & Wagon Co. Ltd. There were seven thirds, three tricompos, and four third brakes. Unlike the Swilly's other carriages, they had rounded corners to the windows, and small horizontal lights between each window and the edge of the roof. The tricomposites were probably arranged 331122 at first, but after second-class travel ended in 1929, the arrangement became 331133. Of the four third brakes, Nos. 25 and 32 had two passenger compartments and capacious luggage-cum-guard's sections, while Nos. 33 and 34 had three passenger compartments and less luggage space. The brake compartments had double glazed doors for luggage, and a single end door for the guard, with a ducket between the two. As with the six-wheelers, reconstruction of the Lancaster bogies gave them vertically matchboarded sides, and on at least one of them (No. 26) the small top lights were removed.

Of the Lancaster coaches, Nos. 28-35 were nominally set aside for the Carndonagh workings and were always referred to by Swilly men as 'the Carn coaches', though they were later used anywhere: thus No. 35 was on a Burtonport train when it was blown off the line at Crolly in February 1923. Indeed, a 1919 Carndonagh guard's report book shows only five out of the eight 'Carn coaches' appearing on trains, while No. 4 of the L & BE series was in regular use.

L & BE carriages. Twelve carriages were supplied by R. Y. Pickering of Wishaw in 1902. The makers lettered them 'No. 1' etc, but the Swilly gave them the prefix 'B'. Nos. 1-5 were thirds, Nos. 6-9 third brakes and Nos. 10-12 tricompos. The third brakes had three passenger compartments and a large luggage/guard's compartment with double glazed doors for luggage and a single guard's door, with a ducket between. The tricomposites were arranged 321123, and 331133 after 1929. As in the L & LS carriages, the third compartments had slatted wood seats, while seconds and firsts were upholstered.

Carriage livery. A writer in 1899 stated that the carriage livery was like that of the London & South Western, i.e. dark brown above and light brown below. This was probably the original colour and is seen in contemporary photographs, but no official written records confirm it.

A 1901 Carndonagh photograph shows Lancaster carriages with white or cream upper panels, and the 1902 Pickering vehicles for the Burtonport line have been stated to have had cream upper panels, and crimson lake below, though works photographs suggest that the carriage ends were a lighter shade, possibly brown. The frames and headstocks appear to be black in these views, and the roofs, footboards and wheel-rims white. At some later stage the carriages were all painted black, lined in red, and finally they were made light grey, unlined, with yellow lettering.

Works photographs of the Pickering/Burtonport carriages show that the classes of compartment were lettered out as 'FIRST', 'SECOND' and 'THIRD', 'LUGGAGE' and 'GUARD' on the doors, between the horizontal mouldings, with 'L. & B.E.R.' between the first and second compartment from each end of the vehicle. After 1929 only 'FIRST' was necessary, and as carriages came through the shops, this was either retained, or replaced by a large 'I' on the lower door panel. Photographs show that the Swilly carriage stock was treated in the same way. Various identifications have been noted; 'L. & L.S.R.' was probably the original, 'L.S.R.' was also used, and in latter years 'LSR' in a diamond was applied.

Carriage lighting and heating. Until 1911 carriages were lit by colza oil lamps. Thereafter, acetylene lighting replaced oil: the generators containing the calcium carbide were metal boxes fixed to one end of each carriage, from which the gas was conveyed by a pipe to each compartment. As may be gathered from the Appendix to the 1920 Working Timetable, the gas generators needed care to avoid waste of carbide. When the old carriages were brought into year-round use during World War II, the old acetylene generators were worn out, and electric lighting was improvised, using heavy bus-type batteries which were put on charge at Derry station as opportunity offered. The system gave as good a light as its two predecessors, and enabled the bulbs to be dimmed by switch when

L & LS CARRIAGE STOCK

No.	Class	Wheels	Compts.	Built	Remarks
1	3	6	5	1884	Damaged collision 26/6/91. To CBPR 6/18—9/21
2	Compo	6	5	1884	Damaged collision 26/6/91. Reb. 5/21
3	Compo	6	5	1884	Arrgt. 33113 (also Nos. 2, 5)
4	3	6	5	1884	
5	Compo	6	5	1884	Damaged collision 26/6/91 as 3rd Damaged ambush 12/1/21
6	3	6	5	1884	Damaged collision 26/6/91
7	3	6	5	1884	Damaged collision 26/6/91. Body reb. 5/29
8	3	6	5	1884	Rebuilt 7/22
9	3	6	5	1884	Damaged collision 26/6/91
10	3	6	5	1884	Rebuilt 2/22
11	3	6	5	1884	
12	3	6	5	1884	Damaged malicious derailment 7/2/23 and Owencarrow 1/25. Rebuilt 1/26
13	3	6	5	1885	Burned in fire, Pennyburn 28/2/23. Rebuilt 10/23
14				1885 ⎫	These 3 vehicles not listed 1925.
15				1885 ⎬	2 compos, 1 was 3rd, accord-
16				1885 ⎭	ing to half-yearly report totals
17	3	6	5	1885	
18	3	6	5	1885	Rebuilt 8/22
19	3	6	5	1895	
20	Trio	6	5	1895	Rebuilt 9/25
21	Compo	6	5	1899	
22	3	6	5	1899	Damaged collision 26/6/91. Referred to as 'compo' 6/91 & 5/22. Burned 28/2/23. Rebuilt as 3rd
23	3	Bgy	6	1901	In use 1937. Converted to hut at Pennyburn later
24	Trio	Bgy	5	1901	
25	3/Bk	Bgy	2	1901	Damaged ambush 12/1/21
26	3	Bgy	6	1901	60 seats. Rebuilt 2/27
27	3	Bgy	6	1901	Heavy repairs 5/21
28	3	Bgy	6	1901	Heavy repairs 11/20. Nos. 28-35 'Carn Coaches'
29	3	Bgy	6	1901	Rebuilt 1/27
30	Trio	Bgy	6	1901	Originally 331122, later 331133 similar arrgt. to No. 31

M

No.	Class	Wheels	Compts.	Built	Remarks
31	Trio	Bgy	6	1901	
32	3/Bk	Bgy	2	1901	Burned 28/2/23. Rebuilt 10/23
33	3/Bk	Bgy	2	1901	Originally 3rd, rebuilt 9/23 as 3/Bk
34	3/Bk	Bgy	2	1901	
35	3	Bgy	6	1901	Burned after derailment 7/2/23. Rebuilt 10/23

Note: Nos. 1-22 were built by Railway Carriage Co. Ltd., Oldbury. Their length over buffers was 31 ft 9 in.

Nos. 23-35 were built by Lancaster Railway Carriage & Wagon Co. Ltd. Their length over buffers was 35 ft 9 in.

Weights and dates of withdrawal and scrapping are not available from official records.

Building dates are derived from stock totals in half-yearly reports.

L & BE CARRIAGE STOCK				
No.	Class	Wheels	Compts.	Remarks
1	3	Bgy	6	Damaged in ambush 12/1/21
2	3	Bgy	6	
3	3	Bgy	6	Heavy repairs 2/18
4	3	Bgy	6	Heavy repairs 6/18. Damaged in Crolly derailment 14/9/25
5	3	Bgy	6	
6	3/Bk	Bgy	3	Derailed Crolly, wind, 7/2/23
7	3/Bk	Bgy	3	Converted to covered wagon/b.van
8	3/Bk	Bgy	3	Slightly damaged, Owencarrow, 1/25
9	3/Bk	Bgy	3	
10	Trio	Bgy	6	Burned 28/2/23. Rebuilt 5/25
11	Trio	Bgy	6	Damaged Owencarrow 1/25
12	Trio	Bgy	6	Damaged Crolly derailment 2/23. Rebuilt 5/25. Heavy repairs 12/27
13	3	Bgy	6	

Note: Nos. 1-12 were built 1903-4 by R. Y. Pickering Ltd.
No. 13 was built 1910 by R. Y. Pickering Ltd.

the trains were in Northern Ireland, where wartime 'black-out' was strictly enforced.

In winter, the Swilly carriage-heating, or the lack of it, was invariably a source of complaint, especially by visitors used to steam heating on main-line trains. The Swilly had none of this, and during its whole career never used steam heating from the engines. Passenger comfort depended on individual hardiness, or on metal footwarmers filled with hot water at the terminus. A stock of old and dilapidated footwarmers came from the Midland Great Western Railway in 1917-18, and the minutes mention the purchase of a further 29 secondhand footwarmers from the CDRJC at 5s each in July 1925.

The L & LS brake van stock began in 1883 with the acquisition of four vehicles (Nos. 1-4) with covered ends, for passenger-train working. In 1892, when the carriages were given continuous vacuum brakes, these vans were also fitted and continued to run as luggage vans. No. 5 brake van, which had open ends, seems to have come in late 1887. The successive reports to the shareholders list six brake vans from 1895 to 1900, but the stock thereafter reverted to five. In the 1925 census, 11 were listed: Nos. 1-5 as above, and Nos. 124, 129-133. The latter were not vacuum fitted but were used until around 1914 on mixed trains with a guard and a brakesman on board. No. 124 was converted to a stores van, vacuum fitted, and renumbered 119 after the original wagon with that number had been scrapped.

The three L & LS *timber trucks* (Nos. 1-3) in the 1925 list appear to have been small, four-wheeled, centre-bolster vehicles, with a handbrake on one side only and not vacuum fitted. The half-yearly, and later annual, reports which group Swilly and Burtonport stocks, show two timber trucks up to 1904, then three until 1913 and four until 1948. These figures are difficult to equate with the fact that Pickering supplied a single, centre-bolster timber truck (No. 61) for the Burtonport line in October 1902, but perhaps conversion or scrapping of one of the earlier vehicles in that year may account for this. The 1948-52 total of seven timber trucks was obtained by the local conversion of old flat wagons.

L & LS and L & BE wagons. From 1887 until 1899 the Swilly's stock of these was made up of 73 open wagons or 'flats', 35 covered and five cattle wagons, a total of 112. By 1912 the combined totals of the two series was 169 open, 105 covered and five cattle wagons.

The official 1925 breakdown gives a relatively complete picture. The Swilly vehicles ran from No. 1 to No. 196; as already stated six of these were brake vans, though by 1925 a second No. 124 was in stock as a covered wagon. Of this total, 8 numbers are vacant (1, 9, 32, 40, 84, 86, 88, 142) having presumably been scrapped by then. A photograph shows No. 1 to have been a timber truck; nothing is known of their history. The remaining Lough Swilly wagons were distributed as shown in the table on page 164.

The Swilly's flats were built with three-plank or four-plank sides.

Flats, falling sides	Nos. 2-5, 7, 8, 11, 12, 14-18, 20-30, 35, 37, 39, 83, 85, 87, 89-91, 93-100, 136-138, 140, 141, 143-146, 148-161, 163-167, 169-178, 186-196 *Total* 90
Flats, centre door	Nos. 13, 31, 33, 34, 36, 80-82, 101-115, 138, 139, 147 *Total* 26
Covered	Nos. 43, 47, 49, 52, 54, 62, 64-66, 69, 71, 74, 75, 116-118, 120-128, 134, 135 *Total* 27
Covered, centre canvas	Nos. 19, 44-46, 48, 50, 51, 53, 55-61, 63, 67, 68, 70, 72, 73, 76, 92, 179-184 *Total* 29
Cattle trucks	Nos. 41, 42, 77-79 *Total* 5
Oil tanks	Nos. 10, 185 *Total* 2
Coal stage	No. 6 (at Burtonport) *Total* 1
	(Three coal stages are listed in the Annual Report for this year)
Stores van	No. 119 *Total* 1
Stone engine	No. 162 (steam powered) *Total* 1
Stone breaker	No. 168 *Total* 1
	(Two stone breakers are listed in the Annual Report)
Total of all types 183	

The latter were listed as 'high-sided' and were then Nos. 13, 15, 31, 33, 34, 36, 80-82, 93, 101-115, 139 and 186. Vacuum-fitted vehicles in 1925 were Nos. 19, 35, 41-79, 92, 116-128, 134, 135, 179-184, 186-190. A travelling crane is shown in the totals after 1936.

Later, the Swilly's wagon stock was extended from No. 197 to No. 208 by the purchase of second-hand vehicles from the Clogher Valley Railway in 1943. Of these, Nos. 201, 206 and 207 were flats, and Nos. 198-200 and 202-205 were covered wagons, while No. 197 was a bogie flat. No. 208 was another bogie flat but came only partly from the Clogher Valley purchases: it was a remarkable wartime Pennyburn production in June 1944, mounting three bodies from Clogher Valley flats on the carriage frame from Carndonagh third No. 23.

Also running were six oil tanks, Nos. 1537-40 of the B.P. Co. and Nos. 3007-8 of the Anglo-American Co., an un-numbered mess and tool van, and three Buda-engined milesmen's trolleys bought in 1931. Some renumbering and reconstruction took place among the Swilly wagons prior to 1925, but the existing files of superintendent's monthly reports do not refer to specific vehicles, so that their history cannot now be traced. Details are largely lacking of the makers' names, though a works photograph shows that No. 189 came from R. Y. Pickering in February 1914. A flat No. 197 was also supplied by Pickering, though as we have seen this number was later taken up by the ex-CVR bogie flat. Nos. 191-196, all flats with falling sides, are known to have been built at Pennyburn, probably during World War 1 when new supplies were restricted.

The L & BE wagons ran from No. 1 to No. 91, and were probably made by R. Y. Pickering between 1902 and 1910. All but three were four-wheeled, and were distributed as follows:

Flats	Nos. 1-15, 69-88 *Total 35*
Covered, centre canvas	Nos. 16-20, 23-25, 28-38, 40-43, 45-51, 53, 54, 56, 58-60 *Total 36*
Covered	Nos. 21, 22, 26, 27, 39, 44, 52, 55, 57, 63-68 *Total 15*
Timber truck	No. 61 *Total 1*
Horse box	No. 62 (the works photograph shows it as No. 61) *Total 1*
Bogie, covered	Nos. 89-91 *Total 3*
Total of all types 91	

The considerably higher ratio of covered to flat wagons in the Burtonport stock reflects the much greater importance of fish traffic on the Extension. The three bogie wagons, Nos. 89-91, were supplied primarily for fish traffic. Wagon livery was grey, with lettering L & LSR or L & BER in white.

The abstracts from the half-yearly reports (to 1912) and the annual reports (after 1912) show the trend of the carriage and wagon stock are shown overleaf.

	1890	1900	1905	1912
Passenger vehicles				
Third class carriages	13	16	25	26
1st/2nd class carriages	5	6	5	5
Tricomposite carriages	—	—	6	6
Brake vans	5	6	5	5
Third/brakes	—	—	7	7
Horse boxes	1	1	2	2
Fish vans	—	—	—	3
Timber & carriage trucks	2	2	3	3
Goods wagons				
Open	73	88	144	169
Covered	34	39	99	105
Cattle trucks	5	5	5	5

	1920	1930	1940	1945	1950	1952
Carriages, 3rd	25	34	26	23	23	23
do., compos.	12	10	6	5	5	4
do., 3rd/brake	7	—	—	—	—	—
Luggage, parcel & brake vans	4	4	1	1	1	1
Horse boxes	1	1	1	1	1	1
Miscellaneous	3	3	3	3	3	3
Open wagons, up to 8 tons	151	151	147	133	69	63
do., 8-12 tons	—	—	—	2	1	1
do., 12-20 tons	—	—	—	1	1	1
Covered wagons, up to 8 tons	107	109	108	101	103	103
Special wagons	—	2	5	3	3	2
Cattle trucks	5	5	5	1	—	—
Rail and timber trucks	4	4	4	4	7	7
Brake vans	7	5	5	5	4	4
Miscellaneous	1	—	4	6	10	11
Mess and tool vans	1	1	1	—	1	1
Stores van	1	1	1	—	—	—
Coal stages	2	3	2	2	1	1
Stone crushers	2	2	—	—	—	—
Travelling crane	—	—	1	1	1	1
Horse	1	—	—	—	—	—

CHAPTER XV

Miscellaneous

THE ROAD SERVICES

Few bus and lorry operators in the British Isles serve such a sparsely-populated district as north Donegal, but in spite of that, the Swilly buses now cover a route mileage three times that of the railway in its prime.

The Swilly's first activity on the roads began in December 1929, when the omnibus service of Mr Barr of Buncrana was bought. In that first month, receipts amounted to £215 and expenditure was £263. In 1930 four further omnibus services were acquired, those of Doherty (Buncrana), Burns (Kilmacrenan), M'Laughlin (Carndonagh) and Kane (Culdaff) and the Company bought more vehicles, having 24 by the end of the year. Reorganisation and expansion began in earnest in 1931 under Mr Whyte's management. The services of Doherty (Moville), Ward Bros (Kerrykeel), Kearney (Carndonagh) and Roberts (Derry) were absorbed, giving the Company a total of 37 buses by December 1931. The first two lorries came in that year.

Under the terms of the Irish Free State Transport Act of 1933, a large number of merchandise services operated by licensed carriers were acquired during 1935, and as a result the lorry fleet rose from four to 56 that year. By the outbreak of World War II, scrapping had reduced the fleet to 41 lorries and 32 buses. Buses remained at 32 during the war, but lorries were added as opportunity permitted, 60 being in use by 1946.

By 1950 the total annual expenditure on the road fleet, 59 lorries, four mail vans and 52 buses, was £191,500, and the receipts £207,500. Of this the goods services contributed about one-third. Similar annual balances have continued since then.

As John McFarland found 80 years ago, in a territory such as north Donegal every possible economy is necessary on both the traffic and engineering sides. Area controllers look after both passenger and goods traffic, and in many places old station buildings are used as local offices. Crews take several of the buses home with

them, and servicing and refuelling is done at places like Letterkenny
and Moville during lay-over periods. Certain routes in the remoter
areas are worked by one-man buses. At Derry, the former railway
engineering shops have been adapted to supplement bus running
sheds erected in 1942, when the original L & LS garage was requisitioned by the U.S. Navy, never to be returned. As far as possible
vehicles based at, and west and north of, Letterkenny, are over-
hauled in area workshops at the old Company station in Letterkenny.

The services cross the Eire border at three approved points with
customs posts: Bridge End (a few miles from Derry city), Muff and
Carrigans. Schedules allow time for customs clearance, but occasional delays are inevitable. Passengers are responsible for clearing
their own luggage through the customs, but generally the officials
are helpful and carry out their checks on the buses. In any case, the
Republic customs men do not check passengers' baggage leaving the
Republic.

Every time a bus crosses the border, the conductor (on behalf of
the driver) has to take a special pass to each of the two customs
posts. The frequency of bus crossings varies widely: the Carrigans
post is comparatively little used, but the busy Bridge End post sees
from 50 to 70 buses pass during a day. As a proportion of the cross-
border movements take place after normal customs hours, the
Company have to pay a large annual sum in supplementary fees.

Although the Swilly tax each vehicle in the country in which it
is normally stationed, they all operate at some time in each country,
and therefore have to be inspected annually by the public service
vehicle inspectors from both Governments. Similarly, both the
driver and the conductors have to hold p.s.v. licences for both
countries. Vehicle insurances must also satisfy dual requirements.
A further financial penalty is the import duty levied on vehicles
brought for the first time into the Republic. This is no less than
150 per cent on second-hand bodies, and is least when chassis or
body is imported in 'knocked-down' condition, to be assembled by
local labour. New buses delivered in recent years have been flat-
engined Leylands, earlier ones with Saunders-Roe bodies, and later
ones with Metroplitan-Cammell-Weymann bodies, knocked down
for assembly in Dublin. The one-man buses are Albion-Nimbus 31
seaters, with bodies built by O'Doherty of Lifford.

In their operating area the Swilly handle nearly all the Republic
Post Office work, mails forming a substantial part of their revenue.
Where a post office is on or close to a bus route, the conductors

deliver and collect bags. From time to time buses are used to carry mails alone, avoiding usually what would otherwise be an empty trip.

The Derry—Buncrana route is by far the busiest of the Company's services, carrying well over a million passengers a year. It services some fine beaches, and on fine summer Sundays buses leave every four minutes.

THE MARINE SERVICES ON LOUGH SWILLY

Lough Swilly was an important shipping centre before the days of the railway, and in fact even before steam ships sailed with emigrants from the Lough to America. Apart from that, there were internal local services between various places on the Lough. During the existence of the railway these marine services passed through four periods of working: 1, 1864-77, charter arrangements with various firms; 2, 1877-1923, worked by Messrs McCrea & McFarland (Lough Swilly Steamship Co. Ltd.); 3, 1923-52, worked by Londonderry & Lough Swilly Railway Co.; 4, from 1952 worked by Mr Brown of Inch Island.

During the first period, arrangements were made with several firms: Andrews & Alexander, Brownlow & Lumsden, James Corry, Robert Smyth, and Green & McCool. It would seem from reference in the minutes that the railway were sometimes responsible for the crews' wages; thus on 2 June 1864 authority was given for the payment of weekly wages of one guinea to C. Toye, helmsman, 12s to deckhand Lockhart, and £1 5s to E. McLaughlin, pilot and captain. These men were probably the crew of P.S. *Vista*, hired from Messrs Andrews & Alexander.

In mid-1864 reference is made to the P.S. *Swilly*, which seems to have been owned at first by Brownlow & Lumsden. In July 1864 two members of the Board were authorised to look out for a 'skilled fireman' for the Swilly steamer. By August 1864 approval was given to the hiring of the P.S. *Alexandra* in accordance with Capt Coppins's telegram of 30 August.

Only the *Swilly* seems to have remained in the Lough for any length of time. By October 1865 it appears to have been in the hands of one Robert Smyth and arrangements were almost completed between the parties when they broke down; a similar agreement was made with James Corry. This only lasted until mid-1866, by which time the *Swilly* was stated to be lying useless, due to bad boilers.

The Derry engineering firm of Messrs Green & McCool appear as ship operators by 1868 and although their relations with the railway were punctuated with a succession of disputes, during which steamer services ceased for a time, they managed to maintain a tolerably regular lough service until 1877. Green & McCool apparently had the *Swilly* repaired before acquiring a second boat. The *Swilly* was old by this time, having been built in Hull in 1849. It is said to have been 82 ft in length, 20 ft beam, 7½ ft draught, gross tonnage 80 and n.h.p. 26. Green & McCool's second vessel may have been the P.S. *Elizabeth*, much larger than its companion and reputed to have been 188 ft in length, 19 ft beam, 6 ft 4 in. draught, 118 tons gross, and n.h.p. 30. The firm ceased to operate by 1877, its principals having died.

From 1877 until 1922 the Lough Swilly shipping was under the control of Messrs McCrea & McFarland, who were synonymous with the Lough Swilly Steamship Co. They may have had the old P.S. *Swilly* at first but replaced it with the ex-steam yacht *Menai* of 41 tons, believed to have lasted until 1883. In 1880 the P.S. *Innishowen*, 120 tons, came to the Lough where it worked until 1912. In 1896, a small 90 ton paddler named the *Kate* was obtained secondhand.

In 1905, a new vessel, the P.S. *Lake of Shadows* (140 tons) was added to McCrea & McFarland's fleet and for the next seven years three boats were at work, until the *Kate* and the *Innishowen* were withdrawn. They were replaced in 1913 by the new, Dartmouth-built T.S.S. *Aberfoyle*. The *Aberfoyle* had a gross tonnage of 100; it served only for two years before being requisitioned by the Admiralty, never to return.

In February 1923 the Lough Swilly Steamship Co. was bought by the L & LS and they took into stock the paddle boat *Lake of Shadows* along with two small motor boats. On 27 May 1923 with a falling tide, the *Lake of Shadows* was stranded on a return Sunday excursion sail from Rathmullan to Fahan.

Under the railway, the decision was speedily taken to operate the marine services by small motor boats and after six years the P.S. *Lake of Shadows* was withdrawn and sold for £15 during 1933. To take over the workings in a more economical fashion came the *Maureen* and the *Inish Isle*, which both lasted from 1934 until 1950. In 1947 the second *Aberfoyle* came into service, being a converted motor launch ex-US Navy.

After 29 years the Railway Company terminated lough services in May 1952, and sold their interests to Mr Brown of Inch Island.

CONCLUSION: DIVIDENDS IN SPITE OF DEPOPULATION

Like its neighbour, the Finn Valley Railway, the Lough Swilly was built into a district that had been suffering progressive depopulation. The London directorate that initiated the Company were soon glad to hand over to a local Board, but still they were unable to make the line pay. Even less successful were the promoters of the Letterkenny Railway, who had hoped to see their line join that of the Swilly. It took the energetic and hard-headed combination of Basil McCrea and John McFarland to make the Lough Swilly Railway a financial success, and yield a dividend of 7 per cent.

Railway construction in the poverty-stricken west of Ireland was fostered by massive Government grants towards the end of the 19th century. Two of these lines were added as Extensions to the Lough Swilly's railway and joined it to the fishery harbour of Burtonport and to the small market town of Carndonagh. By their geographical situation the Extensions were fated never to be profit-making, and while this was fully appreciated by the members of the Swilly's Board, their necessary pursuit of economy brought them into violent conflict with the overseeing Government department. The basic difficulties of the situation were never properly resolved and were confused by the artificial conditions of the 1914-18 war. The end of that conflict brought no peace to the Swilly. The torment of civil war was followed by the imposition of an inter-state frontier across the railway, and that by road competition. The Company's continued existence was only made possible by annual Government grants, which came from both sides of the border. By 1931, under new and energetic management, the Company resolved to base their future on the extension of road services and on the extinction of the railway. In this they differed radically from their neighbour, the County Donegal Railways Joint Committee.

The differing policies of the two concerns originated in their ownerships. That of the Swilly was local, and prepared to adapt for survival. The CDRJC by contrast was an appendage, albeit a lively one, of two large main-line railway companies.

Seen in present-day perspective, the wisdom of the Swilly's rail-to-road policy cannot be doubted. The Company have continued as an efficient, profit-making concern in a countryside that would seem, to cross-Channel operators, decidedly unpromising.

Appendices

1 : LIST OF STATIONS AND HALTS

M. c.		Opened	Closed	Crossing	Water	Block Post
0 . 0	Londonderry Graving Dock	1863	1953			
0 .20	Pennyburn Halt (not public)	1863	1953		W	B
1 .78	Gallagh Road	1880	1924			
2 .53	Harrity's Road	1864	1864			
3 .58	Bridge End	1863	1953	X	W	B
5 .14	Burnfoot	⎰ 1864	1866			
		⎱ 1875	1953			
6 .20	Tooban Junction	⎰ 1864	1868	X	W	B
		⎱ 1883	1953			
7 .40	Trady	1863	1866			
8 .70	Farland	1863	1866		W	
7 . 6	Inch Road	1864	1953			
7 .54	Lamberton's Halt	1927	1948			
9 .17	Fahan	1864	1953		W	B
10.40	Beach Halt	c.1939	c.1948			
11.00	Golf Platform					
	(later Lisfannon Links)	1892	1953			
12.15	Buncrana	1864	1953	X	W	B
14.11	Ballymagan	1901	1935			
15.65	Kinnego Halt (No. 3 Gates)	c.1930	1935			
17.70	Drumfries	1901	1935			
21.40	Meendoran Halt (No. 5 Gates)	c.1930	1935			
23.00	Clonmany	1901	1935	X	W	B
24.32	Ballyliffin	1901	1935			
26.14	Rashenny	1901	1935			
28.00	Carndoagh Halt	c.1930	1935			
30.29	Carndonagh	1901	1935		W	B
9 .22	Carrowen	1883	1953			
12.73	Newtoncunningham	1883	1953	X	W	B
16.57	Sallybrook	1883	1953			
18.44	Manorcunningham	1883	1953			
20.45	Pluck	1883	1953			
24.60	Letterkenny	1883	1953	X	W	B

25.40	Oldtown	1903	1947			
28.49	New Mills	1903	1947			
30. 1	Foxhall	1903	1947			
33.43	Churchill	1903	1947			
37.12	Kilmacrenan	1903	1947	X	W	B
39.50	Barnes Halt (No. 8 Gates)	1927	1940			
45.32	Creeslough	1903	1947	X	W	B
46.46	Dunfanaghy Road	1903	1947			
53.37	Falcarragh	1903	1947			
56.59	Cashelnagore	1903	1947			
62.66	Gweedore	1903	1947	X	W	B
65.79	Crolly	1903	1940			
71.40	Kincasslagh Road	1913	1940			
72.73	Loughmeala (later Dungloe Rd)	1903	1940			
74.36	Burtonport	1903	1940		W	B

Carndonagh halt noted in guard's journal on 24 May 1929 as Campbell's halt.

2 : LIST OF OFFICERS

LONDONDERRY & LOUGH SWILLY RAILWAY

CHAIRMEN—

James Clay 1858
Joseph Cary 1858-61
James T. Macky 1861-85
Bartholomew McCorkell 1885-7
Joseph Cooke 1887-96
Sir John McFarland, Bt. 1896-1917
J. Brice Mullin 1917-23
I. J. Trew Colquhoun 1923-44
Sir Basil A. T. McFarland, Bt. 1944

MANAGERS—

John Dawson 1863-7
Joseph McDonald 1867-9
Fred. Dawson 1883-1901
Robert S. Moore 1901-08
R. T. Wilson 1908-12
Andrew Spence 1912-14 (general managers from 1912)
J. L. Clewes 1914-16
Henry Hunt 1916-31
James J. W. Whyte 1931-67

SECRETARIES—

— Arthur   -1858
Fred. H. Hemming 1858-61
Maurice F. Scott 1907-08
A. H. Stewart 1861-83
Fred. Dawson 1883-1901
Andrew Spence 1901-14 (Joint office with general manager
     from 1912)
J. L. Clewes 1914-16
Henry Hunt 1916-31
James J. W. Whyte 1931-67

TRAFFIC MANAGERS—

R. S. Moore 1901-08
R. T. Wilson 1908-12
John May 1912-16

LOCOMOTIVE SUPERINTENDENTS—

Philip Ellis (driver and fitter) 1862-6
Robert Collins (engineer) 1866-74
C. E. Stewart (engineer) 1874-84
Philip Ellis 1884-90

Thomas Turner 1890-95
F. G. Miller 1895-April 1900
James Stewart (fitter i/c) April-July 1900
John Fisher July 1900-1904
James Conner 1904-05
H. T. Dobbs 1905-06
James Gibson 1906-07
James Baxter 1908-09
Charles H. Swinerd 1909-11
Ingham Sutcliffe 1911-14
C. J. Cotching 1914-May 1915
Ernest Maslin May 1915-Nov. 1918
W. H. Holman (fitter i/c) Nov. 1918-Jan. 1919
P. P. Higgins Jan.-June 1919
W. H. Holman (fitter i/c) June-July 1919
W. Napier 1919-1951
Jas. Armstrong (chief mech. eng.) 1951-

ENGINEERS—

James Bayliss 1852
A. W. Forde (consulting) 1852-55
Sir John & Telford Macneill (consulting) 1860-
Robert Collins 1866-74 (p.way inspector)
Philip Ellis 1875-80 (p.way inspector)
C. E. Stewart 1880-88
Edmund Moore 1888-92
James Cairns 1892-1903
T. A. Hall 1903-06
W. H. Morris 1906-10
Alex. Richardson 1910-12
Norman D. MacKintosh 1912-15
Sidney F. Jones April-July 1916
E. Maslin 1916
— McCann 1916
R. B. Newall 1916-37
R. H. Newall 1937-

LETTERKENNY RAILWAY

ENGINEER—

John Bower 1860-76
F. A. Doyle 1876-7
John Bower 1877-80
Robert Collins 1880-

CHAIRMEN—

A. J. R. Stewart 1860-78
(during the above period Messrs J. F. Grove and J. T. Macky
also acted as chairmen for short periods)
J. T. Macky 1878-85

3 : DIRECTORS

LONDONDERRY & LOUGH SWILLY RAILWAY

Lesley Alexander 1898-1901, T. Edgar Biggar 1902, Alex. Black 1878-94, John Brewster 1910-22, Henry Carrisen 1858-61, Joseph Cary 1858-61, James Clay 1853-8, David M. Colquhoun 1872-92, Isaac Colquhoun 1860-69, I. J. Trew Colquhoun 1913-44, Thos. Colquhoun 1871-1914, James Corscadden 1861-83, 1887-8, Robt. Corscadden 1903-04, Joseph Cooke 1861-96, Henry J. Cooke 1896-1911, John Cross 1853-1861, Edward Doherty 1900-1917, James Garrard 1860-61, David Gillies 1883-7, Saml. Gilliland 1853-78, Philip Hanbury 1853-61, John R. Hastings 1917-52, Chas. Kelly 1919-28, Henry Lecky 1883-5, Alex. Lindsay 1853-8, John Lyon 1860-61, James Thompson Macky 1860-85, Bart. McCorkell 1860-87, Bart. H. McCorkell 1895, Henry J. McCorkell 1887-1923, John McClintock 1898-9, Thompson Macky McClintock 1861-73, Basil McCrea 1898-1907, James McCormick 1928-61, Sir John McFarland 1884-1917, John T. McFarland 1950- , Sir Basil A. T. McFarland 1921- , John McLaughlin (I) 1924-43, John McLaughlin (II) 1958, Joseph McLaughlin 1945-56, J. Brice Mullin 1917-24, John Munn 1861-8, Jonathan Richardson 1861, J. Kelso Reid 1917-21, Jas. A. Piggott 1939-61, William A. Talbot 1898-1913, William D. Porter 1873-84, William H. Thomas 1853-8, Joseph Thornton 1858-61, Frederick C. Towers 1961- , George Tyrrell 1853-8, Daniel Warren 1853-61.

LETTERKENNY RAILWAY

(dates are given where known)

Alex. Black 1880-87, John R. Boyd 1869-?, Edward Clarke ?-1863, Robert Collum, David M. Colquhoun, Joseph Cooke 1863-87, James Corscadden, Jas. P. Grove 1865-78, R. Gunter ?-1863, J. Humphreys 1860-63, Edward Hunter, J. T. Macky 1863-87, John McFarland 1884-7, Bart. McCorkell 1863-87, John Munn 1863-8, Edmund Murphy 1872-80, Robert W. Newton 1869-87, W. Olphert 1861-3, T. Patterson, W. H. Porter, A. J. R. Stewart 1860-78, J. V. Stewart 1860-66, John Thompson 1862-4, William Tillie 1876-?, J. B. Wood.

4 : NOTES ON TICKETS

By C. R. GORDON STUART*

This Company adopted a colour scheme for its tickets that is totally different to any other British or Irish railway, inasmuch as its basic colours for *singles* of first-, second- and third-classes were pink, dark blue and white respectively. On the Carndonagh Extension the tickets were headed 'L & L S Ry (C E)' for a time. The writer has been given to understand that the Burtonport Extension never had any such specially headed tickets, and as yet has never seen any.

Apart from the unique basic colour scheme just mentioned, L & LSR tickets had a very standardised appearance, *returns* originally being all pink for first-class and all blue for second-class, but latterly the *excursions* were yellow and white for first-class and pink and blue for second-class. Special tickets also existed in all classes for such purposes as *sea-bathing*, *golfing* and *Sunday excursions*, which latter generally were in *single* form.

The L & LSR being a line that had seasonal traffic issued a special series of tickets in third-class for *harvestmen* and also *fish-workers*, which were both white, with a red vertical band in the first case and a green vertical band in the latter. They also issued special *rail and steamboat* tickets over to Rathmullan, *via* the Fahan—Rathmullan steamboat service and when the train service was mostly replaced by buses, rail-type tickets were issued at Rathmullan through to Londonderry, which were white, but with no class shown and the word 'BUS' overprinted in red. During the second world war, the train service was restored on sections where the track had not been removed and some interesting third-class *rail and bus singles* appeared to enable the trip to be completed by road.

Excursion tickets on the L & LSR were issued profusely and there was a galaxy of specially printed excursion tickets in single form, whose many colours were most pleasing; they were all of third-class, as only *Sunday excursions* were issued in both first- and third-classes.

The Company also had quite a novel colour for *dog* tickets, which was green and white, whilst *perambulator* tickets were buff with a red 'P' overprinted; *cycle* tickets were pink, similar to the first-class colour. Mention must also be made of some interesting Bell Punch Company's tickets that were used on the steamboats; they were also issued at halts by the guard. Some of these Bell Punch issues are blank tickets which require the destination to be written in by hand.

*This Appendix is reproduced, with minor alterations, from H. Fayle's book *Narrow Gauge Railways of Ireland*, to which it formed an Appendix. The author is indebted to Mr Fayle and to Mr C. R. Gordon Stuart for permission to use it.

N

5: RELEVANT ACTS OF PARLIAMENT

1.	27-7-1838	An Act for draining and embanking certain Lands in Lough Swilly & Lough Foyle, &c.	1 & 2 V., c.87
2.	17-8-1843	Amending Act to (1)	6 & 7 V., c.100
3.	27-7-1846	Amending Act to (1) and (2)	9 & 10 V., c.298
4.	28-6-1853	Lough Swilly Railway Act 1853	16 & 17 V., c.54
5.	-1854	Londonderry Port & Harbour Act 1854	17 & 18 V., c.177
6.	1-8-1859	Lough Swilly (Deviation) Act 1859	22 & 23 .V., c.50
7.	3-7-1860	Letterkenny Railway Act 1860	23 & 24 V., c.99
8.	22-7-1861	Lough Swilly Railway (Buncrana Ext.) Act 1861	24 & 25 V., c.161
9.	13-7-1863	Letterkenny Railway Act 1863	26 & 27 V., c.96
10.	25-7-1864	Lough Swilly Railway (Extension) Act	
11.	11-6-1866	Letterkenny & Londonderry & Lough Swilly Companies Act 1866	29 V., c.60
12.	24-7-1871	Letterkenny Railway Act 1871	34 & 35 V., c.148
13.	30-6-1874	Letterkenny Railway (Extension of Time) Act 1874	37 & 38 V., c.148
14.	- -1874	Londonderry Port & Harbour Act 1874	37 & 38 V., c.159
15.	13-7-1875	Letterkenny Railway Act 1876	39 & 40 V., c.110
16.	22-7-1878	Letterkenny Railway Act 1878	41 & 42 V., c.192
17.	29-6-1880	Letterkenny Railway Act 1880	43 & 44 V., c.23
18.	3-7-1882	Lough Swilly Railway (Further Powers) Act 1882	45 & 46 V., c.79
19.	24-7-1882	Londonderry Port & Harbour Act 1882	45 & 46 V., c.142
20.	25-7-1898	Tramways Order in Council (Ireland) L. & L.S. (L. to B. Ext.) Rly. Confirmation Act 1898	61 & 62 V., c.101
21.	21-11-1918	Londonderry & Lough Swilly Rly Act 1918	
22.	7-8-1924	Londonderry & Lough Swilly Rly Act 1924	

6: SOME VERSE

The Swilly had its full share of attention by amateur writers of verse, and although they scarcely reached the standard of the late Percy French's lines on the West Clare Railway, it is believed that they should be recorded. Some were published in local newspapers, others as 'broad-sheets' which were sold at the doors or at street-corners.

THE SWILLY

There's a railway in Derry, the Swilly, you know,
That is famed for going exceedingly slow.
It leaves Londonderry about ten minutes late
And if they don't watch it may run through the gate.
In five minutes more a whistle is heard
And old Lizzie Harkin is getting prepared.
Proceeding along and turning a bend
The train shortly reaches the station Bridge End.
At the next stop a man in a suit navy-cut
Calls out that the train has arrived at Burnfoot.
(Unfortunately incomplete. Lizzie was the station agent at Gallagh Road.)

THE BUNCRANA TRAIN

Some people like to have a drive
Whilst others like a row,
Young people getting up in life
A-courting they will go.
But if the evening does keep fine
And does not threaten rain,
Sure I'd prefer a trip to Fahan
On the 'Buncrana Train'.

Chorus:
For Crockett he's the driver,
And Bonner is the guard,
And if you have a ticket
All care you can discard.
Let you be fop or 'summer swell',
To them it's all the same,
For every man must pay his fare
On the 'Buncrana Train'.

For localists, provocalists,
And those that like to sing,
I'm sure McGarvey he'll be there
To play the Highland Fling.
As for singing or for dancing
To them it's all the same,
For he's the sole 'musicianer'
On the 'Buncrana Train'.
Chorus

We pass Bridgend, reach Burnfoot,
And there we give a call
To view that ancient city
And its Corporation Hall.
The King of Tory Island
Is a man of widespread fame,
His Royal Carriage is attached
To the 'Buncrana Train'.
    Chorus

We go to Fahan to have a 'dip'
And stroll along the strand,
Then up the road to have a cup
Of coffee at the Stand.
The Barmaid she is charming,
With her you can remain
Until it's time for to go back
On the 'Buncrana Train'.
    Chorus

(This was published in 1898 in the *Derry Journal*, and it enjoyed considerable popularity as a sing-song of a summer evening among railway trippers from Derry.)

THE VIADUCT DISASTER

On a wild and stormy winter's night,
The little train did steam,
Adown past Kilmacrenan,
And Lurgy's purling stream.
She passed along down through the Gap,
The Owencarrow she passed by,
Until she reached the hills of Doe,
Beneath an angry sky.

A sudden gust came from above;
Two carriages were swept o'er,
Three passengers there met their death,
Leaving hearts both sad and sore.
One other soul did pass away,
Her race on earth is done,
She died in Letterkenny,
At the rising of the dawn.

A band of noble heroes,
Came from far and near;
They worked to save the wounded,
With neither dread nor fear.
Bold lads from Kilmacrenan,
And from the vales of Doe,
Worked hard and sore together,
In that valley full of woe.

Near the village of Falcarragh,
There are hearts both sad and sore,
God help that distressed family,
On the Isle of Arranmore.
I hope and trust the wounded
Will soon be strong again—
That they will all recover
From all their grief and pain.

God help that little family
Living up beside the Gap,
They lost their loving father
In that unfortunate mishap.
I can't mention individuals,
But must give praise to one and all,
Who helped in the disaster
'Mid the hills of Donegal.

The officials of the Railway,
Worked hard with craft and skill;
Each one did play a noble part
Their duties to fulfil—
To assist the sufferers in distress,
In their lonely, weary plight.
Long will our memories wander back,
To that stormy winter's night.

(Published as an undated broad-sheet, written by D. Hay.)

Acknowledgments and Sources

The writing of this book could only have been undertaken knowing that I could depend upon the guidance of many people who had an intimate and specialist knowledge of the Swilly. Throughout, I have been most fortunate in being freely granted access to the Company's records of a century of activity.

The late Sir Basil McFarland, Bt, chairman of the Company, took a close personal interest in the work, and permitted me to consult the papers of his late father dealing with the Swilly and Letterkenny companies.

The long association with the Company of the manager and secretary the late Mr James Whyte, J.P., made him a target for many of my questions, and he most generously gave much effort and time in answering them and in helping me during my visits to Pennyburn. There must also be mentioned Messrs S. H. Bell and J. J. Brady and other members of the railway staff, without whose knowledge the story would have lacked many details.

Information on locomotives and their builders came from the borough librarians of Middlesborough and Stockton-on-Tees, and from the chief draughtsmen of Messrs Andrew Barclay, Sons & Co. Ltd, Kilmarnock, and of the Stephenson works of the English Electric Co. Ltd, Darlington.

Space allows merely the listing of the names of others who have assisted me: Messrs S. J. Carse, H. C. Casserley, R. N. Clements, Hedley Connell, David J. Dickson, H. Fayle, P. Flanagan, E. T. R. Herdman, R. H. Inness, H. S. Irvine, G. R. Mahon, P. Mallon, I. S. Pearsall, R. N. Redman, J. W. P. Rowledge, I. Scrimgeour, B. S. T. Simpson, David L. Smith, D. Stirling, H. P. Swan, J. S. Watt, Patrick B. Whitehouse.

Chisholm, A. J. (1899) The Londonderry & Lough Swilly Railway. *Railway Mag.*, **5,** 461.
(1903) The Letterkenny & Burtonport Railway. *Railway Mag.*, **13,** 120.
(1903) Ten-wheeled locomotive for the Letterkenny & Burtonport Railway. *Engineering* (24 April).
Shrubsole, E. (1908) *Picturesque Donegal* (GNRI Tourist Guide).
Livesey, R. M. (1912) Rolling stock on the principal Irish narrow-gauge railways. *Proc. Inst. Mech. Eng.*, 559 (and in *Engineering*, 2 Aug.).

(1917) Report of the Commissioners of Public Works in Ireland to the Lord Lieutenant on the L & LS (Letterkenny to Burtonport Extension) Railway, with Appendix by J. Tatlow (pp. 38).

(1919) Londonderry & Lough Swilly Railway. *Railway Mag.*, **44**, 73.

(1919) L & LSR—The Railway Position. Memorandum to the Proprietors.

(1922) Cmd. 10. *Report of the Railway Commission in Northern Ireland.* H.M.S.O., Belfast.

(1922) *Irish Railways. Report of the Commission appointed by Provisional Government.* Dail Eireann Papers, S.O., Dublin.

(1923) A novel excursion handbill. *Railway Gaz.*, **39**, 168.

Ward, W. (1933) Railway Stamps of the British Isles. *Railway Mag.*, **73**, 301.

(1934) Report of the County Donegal Transport Committee. S.O., Dublin.

Jackson, W. N. (1936) Replacing a railway—the L & LS system. *Railway Mag.*, **78**, 313.

Leebody, H. A. (1939) Long ago on an Irish railway, *Railway Mag.*, **84**, 335.

Fayle, H. (1945) *Narrow Gauge Railways of Ireland.*

Longbottom, K. (1949) By goods train to Gweedore. *Railway Mag.*, **95**, 353.

Prosser, O. H. (1951) The Londonderry & Lough Swilly Railway. *Trains Illustrated*, **4**, 416.

(1951) Serving a thinly populated countryside by road. *Modern Transport*, **65**, No. 1684, p. 7 and No. 1685, p. 5.

Gallagher, P. (1952) *My story—Paddy the Cope.*

Celkin, C. A. (1952) History of Public Transport in Donegal. *Donegal Annual*, **2**, No. 2, 406.

Patterson, E. M. (1953) The Londonderry & Lough Swilly Railway. *Trains Illustrated*, **6**, 469.

Patterson, E. M. (1953) Exit—the Londonderry & Lough Swilly Railway. *Railway World*, **14**, 61.

Casserley, H. C. (1953) Closure of the Londonderry & Lough Swilly Railway. *Railway Mag.*, **99**, 701.

McNeill, D. B. (1956) Ulster Tramways and Light Railways. *Transport Handbook No. 1*, Museum & Art Gallery, Belfast.

Edwards, R. D. & Williams, T. D. (1956) *The Great Famine.*

(1957) Buses put railway company in the black. *Leyland Journal*, **17**, 400.

(1957) *Report of the Committee of Inquiry into Internal Transport.* S.O., Dublin.

Whitehouse, P. B. (1957) *Narrow Gauge Album.*

Carse, S. J. and Murray, D. (1957) The Londonderry & Lough Swilly Railway. *Journ. Irish Rly. Record Soc.*, 4, 247.

O'Loan, J. (1959) Land reclamation down the years. *Journ. Eire Dept. Agric.*, **55**, 29.

Lambden, W. (1960) Running under two flags. *Bus & Coach*, **32**, 150.

McNeill, D. B. (1960) Coastal Passenger steamers and inland navigations in the North of Ireland. *Transport Handbook No. 2*, Museum & Art Gallery, Belfast.

Patterson, E. M. (1961) The Irish narrow gauge—its growth and decay. *Railway Mag.*, **107**, 75 & 169.

Patterson, E. M. (1962) The Donegal derailments. *Railway World*, **23**, 222.

Patterson, E. M. (1962) *The County Donegal Railways.*

Mahon, G. R. (1963) Irish Railways in 1860. *Journ. Irish Railway Record Soc.*,

Half Yearly Reports of the L & LSR and LR, up to the end of 1912.
Annual Reports of L & LSR, from 1913.
Bradshaw's Railway Manual, Shareholders' Guide and Directory. Various Editions.
Minutes of Board Meetings of L & LSR and LR.
Working and Public Timetables of L & LSR.
Appendix to Working Timetable, L & LSR, April 1920.
Files of *Londonderry Sentinel*, *Derry Journal* and *Derry Standard*.
Tourist Programmes, L & LSR.
Board of Trade: Reports of Railway Accidents.

THE ILLUSTRATIONS

The author is grateful for permission to use photographs as follows:

Mr H. C. Casserley, plates 1, 20, 21, 27, 35, 39, 40, 43, 44, 57; Dr I. S. Pearsall, plates 2, 7, 9, 11, 13, 18, 19, 67; Mr W. A. Camwell, plates 3, 6, 32, 33, 34, 42; Londonderry & Lough Swilly Railway, plates 4, 45, 46, 63, 64, 65, 69; Mr G. R. Mahon, plates 5, 48 (and from a contemporary postcard), plate 24; National Library of Ireland (Lawrence Collection), plates 15, 16, 17, 25, 37, 41; Mr R. G. Oakley, plate 22; Mr H. S. Irvine, plates 26, 28, 68; Mr D. H. Ballantyne, plates 30, 58; Mr C. L. Fry, plates 36, 53, 62; Mr J. J. Brady, plate 47; Mr H. Fayle, plates 49, 50; Messrs Andrew Barclay Sons & Co. Ltd, plate 52; Mr R. G. Jarvis, plate 54; Messrs R. W. Pickering Ltd (per Historical Model Railway Society), plates 59, 60, 61; Mr R. N. Clements, plate 66.

The remainder of the photographs are taken by the author, or are from his collection.

Special thanks are due to Mr Peter C. Allen for permission to reproduce the painting by Mr C. Hamilton Ellis which forms the frontispiece.

Index

Illustrations are indicated by heavy type

Wages, 23, 24, 30, 31, 60, 61, 68, 72, 82, 91, 94
Wagons, 41, 59, 102, 136, 163-167, **plates 60-62**
Wagstaffe, W., 14; & Brassey, 14
War (1914-18), 68, 81, 82; (1939-45), 96, 98, 99; (civil), 84, 87
Water supply, 62-64, 102

Waterside station, 37, 47
Whyte, James J. W., 94, 101, 174
Wind, derailments by, 87, 92, 117, 137-139, **plates 45-47**
Wood as fuel, 99, 100
Working conditions, 31
Workshops, 64, 68, 72, 76, 83, 87